"If there is a narcissist in your life, I highly recommend this book! How narcissists behave always makes sense once you understand their thinking. The way you habitually respond to narcissists always makes sense once you understand your own thinking. This valuable book offers great insight and concrete suggestions for changing your thinking and responses so you can interact with narcissists more effectively, whether you're a family member, intimate, friend, coworker, or therapist."

> —**Judith Beck, PhD**, president of the nonprofit Beck Institute for Cognitive Behavior Therapy, and author of *Cognitive Behavior Therapy*

"*Disarming the Narcissist* in its new edition continues to be a useful guide for anyone doing therapy with a narcissist, or even for those in a relationship with such a person. In this valuable book, we learn to understand the mental schema of a narcissist, and the appropriate interpersonal neurobiology that makes it possible to have hope that we can both understand and survive these very difficult relationships. The book is an essential guide for this widespread problem."

> —**John M. Gottman, PhD**, author of *The Seven Principles for Making Marriage Work*

"Wendy Behary is my go-to therapist when I need information about people with narcissistic personality disorder (NPD), or how they interact with family members. In this new edition, Wendy shows you why you feel so lonely and misunderstood in these relationships, and why you keep your own needs tucked away. Whether you decide to stay in this relationship or leave, the insights Wendy Behary provides make this an essential book for anyone in a relationship with a narcissist."

> —**Randi Kreger**, coauthor of *Stop Walking on Eggshells*, and author of *Stop Walking on Eggshells for Parents*

"The latest edition of *Disarming the Narcissist* provides up-to-date and practical guidance for not only understanding the problem of narcissism, but also a discerning road map for navigating the solution. This book will be a stabilizing and highly recommended resource for anyone who has ever stood in the confusing wake a narcissist leaves."

—**Jill Manning, PhD**, licensed marriage and family
therapist, researcher, and author of *What's the Big Deal about Pornography?*

Praise for the second edition of
Disarming the Narcissist:

"Wendy Behary has dedicated decades to understanding narcissism, both as a clinician and a scholar. In *Disarming the Narcissist*, she distills these hard-won insights into a very readable form. This book is a terrific resource for those looking to better understand narcissism."

—**W. Keith Campbell, PhD**, professor in the department
of psychology at the University of Georgia, and coauthor
of *The Narcissism Epidemic*

disarming
the
narcissist

THIRD EDITION

Surviving & Thriving
with the **Self-Absorbed**

WENDY T. BEHARY, LCSW

New Harbinger Publications, Inc.

Publisher's Note

This publication is designed to provide accurate and authoritative information in regard to the subject matter covered. It is sold with the understanding that the publisher is not engaged in rendering psychological, financial, legal, or other professional services. If expert assistance or counseling is needed, the services of a competent professional should be sought.

Distributed in Canada by Raincoast Books

NEW HARBINGER PUBLICATIONS is a registered trademark of New Harbinger Publications, Inc.

New Harbinger Publications is an employee-owned company.

Cover design by Amy Shoup; Interior design by Michele Waters; Acquired by Tesilya Hanauer

Library of Congress Cataloging-in-Publication Data

Names: Behary, Wendy T., author.
Title: Disarming the narcissist : surviving and thriving with the self-absorbed / Wendy Behary.
Description: 3rd edition. | Oakland : New Harbinger Publications, 2021. | Revised edition of the author's Disarming the narcissist, [2013] | Includes bibliographical references.
Identifiers: LCCN 2021011943 | ISBN 9781684037704 (trade paperback)
Subjects: LCSH: Narcissism. | Interpersonal relations.
Classification: LCC BF575.N35 B44 2021 | DDC 155.2/32--dc23
LC record available at https://lccn.loc.gov/2021011943

Printed in the United States of America

26   25   24

10 9 8 7 6 5 4

FSC
www.fsc.org
MIX
Paper | Supporting responsible forestry
FSC® C008955

This is dedicated to Poppy, a true knight in shining armor.
And to Momma, the artist of unconditional love.

Contents

Foreword   vii

Preface   xi

Introduction   1

1   Framing the Situation: Toward an Understanding of Narcissism   11

2   Understanding the Anatomy of Personality: Schemas and the Brain   35

3   Getting Captured: Identifying Your Personal Traps   59

4   Overcoming the Obstacles: Communication Pitfalls, Snags, and Glitches   75

5   Paying Attention: Facing Difficult Encounters with a Narcissist   93

6   Addressing Perilous and Hypersexual Narcissism: The Challenges of Shame, Trust, and Betrayal Trauma   109

7   Using Empathic Confrontation: A Winning Strategy for Interpersonal Effectiveness   129

8   Co-Parenting with a Narcissist: Protecting Your Children and Supporting Their Wellness   161

9   Making the Most of a Difficult Situation: Seven Gifts of Communication with a Narcissist   187

Acknowledgments   207

Resources   211

References   217

Foreword

Over the years, one of the most common issues that my clients have brought into therapy is how to deal with the self-centered, egotistical behavior of narcissistic partners. These clients almost always feel frustrated, angry, demeaned, and helpless over the almost total lack of sensitivity and empathy their partners show for their needs and feelings. I myself often sit in sessions in disbelief as I hear story after story describing the degree of selfishness these clients have to put up with. So often my clients can't seem to find the strength to either leave or stand up to the narcissists they fell in love with years ago.

I am so excited that my close friend and colleague Wendy Behary has written this definitive book on dealing with narcissists to help the countless number of people who, like my clients, try to live or work with narcissists on a daily basis. While there are several other self-help books on this topic, *Disarming the Narcissist* addresses the issue with great sophistication, depth, and compassion, and offers highly effective strategies for change. Wendy has devoted years of clinical practice to the specialized treatment of narcissists and their partners, making her the perfect author to tackle this very difficult and resistant problem.

Wendy draws on two fields of science and therapy to help the reader better understand and deal with narcissism: schema therapy and interpersonal neurobiology. Schema therapy is an approach I and my colleagues have been developing over the past twenty years to help therapists, clients, and others better understand the deep emotional themes, or schemas, that begin when we are children and eventually lead most of us to engage in repetitive and self-destructive life patterns. I first presented these ideas for the general reader in *Reinventing Your Life*.

Disarming the Narcissist extends the concepts of schema therapy into work with narcissism and includes fresh insights and perspectives that I had never envisioned before reading this book. Wendy provides a wonderful explanation of how schemas, like defectiveness and emotional deprivation, affect our lives in dramatic ways. Her unique contributions to schema therapy lead us to a deeper understanding of the narcissists in our lives, as well as show us how to overcome our own "demons" that keep us from dealing effectively with narcissistic partners, parents, friends, and colleagues.

I am pleased that Wendy has gone so far beyond the clichés and simplistic advice that many other books and therapists offer. There are no simple answers or techniques when it comes to changing narcissism. You will have to delve into this book and work hard to truly understand the wealth of material presented here, but the rewards will be commensurate with your effort. You will learn about the different categories of narcissists, the range of strategies that narcissists so skillfully employ to disarm you and even convince you that you are to blame for their complaints, and the importance of empathic confrontation as a method of communicating with and standing up to narcissists. Wendy offers invaluable suggestions on ways to develop and sustain compassion for narcissists, even when you are being mistreated, and on how to create enough leverage to convince a narcissist to change. *Disarming the Narcissist* also provides rich case examples that bring this approach to life.

If you put in the time required to understand the insights Wendy describes and practice the techniques she offers, you will, probably for the first time, have a set of tools that shift the odds in your favor in your relationship. You will have a newfound confidence that you know how to respond when your partner humiliates you in front of friends and family members or says things like, "You're so stupid if you can't see that my way is the only intelligent one."

I want to conclude by emphasizing a point that Wendy makes repeatedly in this book—a point that is central to schema therapy. As with any other personality problem, we need to approach narcissists and those who live with them in a compassionate way. Most narcissists are not "evil" or "bad" at a deeper level, no matter how they treat us. If you can learn to assert your rights while simultaneously working hard to reach the vulnerable, lonely core of the narcissist in your life, you stand a much better chance of bringing out the side of your partner that can love and care for you.

I know of no better way to achieve this compassionate road to change than to start reading *Disarming the Narcissist* now. As Wendy says in her conclusion, "The self-help journey can be both lonely and arduous." But the dramatic changes in your relationship will usually more than repay your efforts.

I recommend this outstanding book to anyone who lives with, works with, or treats narcissists—including their partners, work associates, family members, and therapists.

> —Jeffrey Young, PhD
> Director, Cognitive Therapy Center and
> Schema Therapy Institute of New York
> Faculty Member, Department of Psychiatry,
> Columbia University
> Founder, International Society of
> Schema Therapy

Preface

If you are in a relationship with someone who exhibits the traits of a narcissistic individual, don't think twice before you read this book. In *Disarming the Narcissist*, Wendy Behary offers a practical tool kit that gives us insights into how we can manage the emotional challenges of relating to someone who does not relate to us: the narcissistic individual.

This gem of a how-to survival guide is filled with useful tips informed by two branches of science: the cognitive science view of how the mind is organized around schemas, and my own field—interpersonal neurobiology. Schemas are generalized filters that bias our perceptions and alter our thinking. For two decades, the author has immersed herself in schema therapy and treatment of those with narcissism as their major issue in psychotherapy. Using this science background and her practical experience as a therapist, Wendy Behary walks us through easy-to-understand explanations of how the mind of a narcissist works. We come to see the schemas that organize how a narcissist sees the world, and how that perspective is often devoid of interest in the internal world of others.

Interpersonal neurobiology examines the connections among relationships, the mind, and the brain. Our professor of how-to-get-along-with-a-narcissist, Wendy Behary, has been studying this field intensively with me for many years, and she has deftly applied it to her own area of expertise in dealing with these individuals who lack the knack of empathy. The circuits in the brain that enable us to imagine the internal subjective experience—the mind—of another person may not be well developed or easily accessed in the narcissist. "*Mindsight*" is our capacity to see the mind itself, in ourselves and in others, and in narcissists, it is often poorly developed. Therefore, relationships with such an individual will feel lopsided: conversations and interactions are all about the other person, not about you or the two of you as a "we."

This lack of empathy in a relationship affects the social circuits of the brain that help create an integrated sense of balance and well-being. Such an imbalance can make you feel isolated and alone. Your mind may become incoherent, and your usual sense of vitality drained. The reaction to such feelings can depend on your own makeup: You may become angry and frustrated, or sullen and withdrawn. Or you may find yourself feeling ashamed, as if you have done something wrong and deserve such an experience of being ignored. In these and other common responses, the relationship with a narcissistic individual creates a cascade of neural reactions that are far from the mental well-being associated with coherence of mind and empathy and compassion in relationships. This is a form of stress that you deserve to reduce in your life, even if you cannot change the other person. The knowledge embedded in the pages of this book can serve as a powerful means to help you deal with this stress through insight and information. If you're in any sort of close relationship with a narcissist, you may be in dire need of new ways to understand the situation and respond—for the sake of the health of your mind, your brain, and your relationships.

Fortunately, the advice in this book will guide you through the challenges of both surviving and optimizing a relationship with someone who initially has so little to give, but who often takes so much. At the very least, this guide will help you understand the mechanisms of mind and brain that are at work in your relationship. This alone will help a great deal. But even more, the suggestions here offer the hope of change. With these science-based practical ideas, you may actually open the door to a new way of being—both for you and for the narcissist in your life. Taking the time to dive into these pages and work with the ideas presented will be worth its weight in gold. If relating to a narcissist presents challenges in your life, why not start now? Turn the page and start to learn how you can improve your life.

—Daniel J. Siegel, MD
Author of *Mindsight*, *The Mindful Brain*, and
The Developing Mind
Coauthor of *The Whole-Brain Child* and
Parenting from the Inside Out
Clinical Professor of Psychiatry, UCLA School
of Medicine

Introduction

Too often we enjoy the comfort of opinion
without the discomfort of thought.

—John F. Kennedy

Because you're reading this book, you're likely in a relationship with a narcissist, whose excessive self-centeredness and sense of entitlement have hurt both you and the relationship time and time again. The useful information, illuminating exercises, and effective strategies in this book can help you understand the narcissist in your life and how you might foster positive changes in your relationship. First, though, let's take a quick look at both our growing awareness of narcissism and the role empathy has to play in healing relationships afflicted by narcissism.

An Era of Narcissism

In recent years, stories highlighting the offensive behaviors of celebrities, sports superstars, and politicians have cast a spotlight on self-serving lifestyles and a "rules don't apply to me" sense of entitlement. Terms such as "narcissism," "sex addiction," and "lack of empathy" have appeared in many headlines (boosting my book sales, thank you very much!).

Once limited to mental health settings, these expressions are joining the lexicon of everyday conversation—from social media sites to kitchen tables—across the globe. As the term "narcissism" has become more widely used and understood, people are pleased and relieved to finally have a description that fits their self-absorbed partner, friend, boss, or family member.

When *Disarming the Narcissist* was first released in 2008, there was little written on the subject for the general reader. The book offered a profile of narcissism and strategies that loved ones might use when dealing with a narcissist. I wrote the book largely in response to people who had expressed a genuine caring for and desire to understand the narcissist in their lives, despite the challenges—people who wanted to encourage change while getting their own needs met. It was also for those who were attempting to set limits, planning to exit a relationship, or struggling with the aftermath of a relationship with a narcissist—perhaps through co-parenting or by simply trying to recapture their self-worth.

Given the surge of publicity surrounding narcissism, it isn't surprising that a host of books on this subject have emerged in recent years. Nevertheless, *Disarming the Narcissist* continues to present a unique approach to the challenges of dealing with a narcissist, offering a comprehensive explanation of narcissism and reasonable navigational tools while still recognizing that transformation is likely to be limited with this complicated personality type.

The Wisdom of Empathy

This book's approach sometimes raises the ire of my colleagues, clients, and readers as they struggle to integrate their mindful hearts into the matter. Some say my book promotes too soft a touch with narcissists and that there is no hope for change with these magisterial maniacs. I understand; after all, people often find themselves shortchanged, frustrated, or dangerously threatened in interactions with narcissists, even after using all the tools of empathic confrontation and limit setting outlined in this book.

Yet potential solutions to this difficult quandary exist. To gather and maintain momentum with a narcissist, you must set forth meaningful consequences—something I'll discuss when we get to empathic confrontation. Here is another area of misunderstanding I will discuss in detail: What, exactly, is empathy, and how could it possibly apply to narcissists?

A tattered heart and eroded hope may not allow for the patience and effort required to experiment with different approaches. Let's face it: It takes more than flawless elocution and carefully crafted language to bring about results. It takes leverage, persistence, an understanding of what you're up against, and a readiness to enforce consequences. For the therapist, it takes the laser-sharp focus of an Olympic athlete, fit emotional muscles, energetic endurance, and the capacity to be vulnerable—to be real, not just nice and not just smart.

Most books on narcissism urge you to *run, don't walk* away from the me-me-me madman or the vainglorious vamp. But as I've learned while facilitating support groups for those dealing with a narcissist, it isn't so easy when the narcissist is your spouse, someone you've dedicated decades of your life to, or the parent of your children. He probably isn't someone you're prepared to hand your kids over to every other weekend. Nor is it so easy when she's your boss or your eldest daughter, and you aren't prepared to exit your job or lose contact with your grandchildren.

The narcissist may be someone you love and understand, someone who captures your heart—albeit in brief moments when his vulnerability and humanness manage to sneak out of an oversized ego to show up as warm and caring. Sadly, it's always just a matter of time before he appears bored and disinterested. As quickly as he showed up, he slips away again. And you may wonder: *Does he carry you with him in his mind? Is the representation accurate? Does he get who you are, what you need, and what it feels like to be in your skin?* This brings me back to empathy, a term that's particularly puzzling in the context of narcissism. I get a lot of questions about empathy, especially these:

- Isn't "empathy" just another word for "compassion"?

- How can one have empathy for a narcissist?

- Can a narcissist ever truly experience what happens inside another person's skin?

Some of the brightest thinkers, including journalists, psychologists, researchers, political analysts, anthropologists, and even wordsmiths, investigate empathy—from studying mirror neurons to pondering moral consciousness. Without empathy, how can people predict the future, view themselves in comparison to others, and hold the world in their mind?

In response to readers' and clients' quandaries, and incorporating new findings on this topic, the second edition of *Disarming the Narcissist* added more material on empathy, including how empathy promotes emotional stability. The second edition also added new material on the female narcissist, in response to a significant number of readers who wrote to me about their struggles with narcissistic women.

The second edition recognized that sometimes the best option is to end the relationship. The third edition has a chapter dedicated to exit strategies. This new content addresses the risks and dangers of living with narcissists who demonstrate hazardous behaviors such as aggression, unremitting addictions (including to pornography, infidelity, gambling, and substances), and a missing moral compass combined with remorselessness and an elevated sense of entitlement.

In this third edition of *Disarming the Narcissist*, I am pleased to once again respond to readers' requests for more content related to important issues: (1) the hypersexuality of narcissists, sexual addiction, and the consequential hardship of experiencing, and dealing with, *betrayal trauma*; (2) co-parenting with a narcissist—both from inside the marriage and from separate homes; and (3) finding an effective divorce attorney who is narcissism-savvy and fluent in the art of mediating or litigating with a narcissistic counterpart.

Indelible Imprints

My interest in narcissism was seeded by unforgettable experiences with very difficult clients in my early years of practicing psychotherapy. Armed with only a hazy residue of information on the subject from graduate and postgraduate studies, and a novice's enthusiasm for the psychology of relationships, I wasn't adequately prepared for dealing with narcissistic people. I found myself flustered, fumbling, and defensive when working with these clients. They could push my buttons like no one else could.

One of my first encounters with a narcissistic client came while I was an intern. My job was to conduct interviews with couples in the process of divorcing and assist them in resolving disputes on matters of child custody and visitation. Let's just say that diving into frigid waters headfirst from the highest cliff would have been benign by comparison.

My baptism by fire began when an attractive forty-five-year-old man arrived to our session ahead of his soon-to-be ex-wife. He glared at me—a twenty-five-year-old woman in a navy blue suit sporting a clipboard, a welcoming handshake, and barely ripened clinical expertise. He took a seat, sighed, looked at his watch, and then asked, "Just exactly how damn long will this take?" Before I could stutter a response, he asked, "When will the counselor be arriving?" I am pretty good at staving off color rising toward my face, so with a forced smile I replied, "I am the counselor." He rolled his eyes, threw back his head with disapproval, and turned to stare out the window, impatiently tapping a finger on the arm of his chair.

In the uncomfortable silence, I first thought about a career in floral design, but I then told myself, *Wendy, this is a disgruntled man who is going through a divorce. He has a lot on his mind. He's just upset. You can handle it. You have your inventory of questions, you are rehearsed, and you have an order from the court. Yes, you are uncomfortable with bullies, but you will get through it. You know how to focus, and you are sensitive to your clients.*

His wife arrived about five minutes later—seemed like days. She was a lovely woman and was immediately apologetic for being late. She introduced herself and said hello to her husband, who didn't respond, and took a seat. I proceeded to open the session by reviewing the information I had received from the court. He continued to sigh heavily, staring up at the ceiling. She nodded, affirming that all the information was correct.

The document stated the reasons for court-ordered mediation: the couple could not agree on who should have primary custody of their three children. He proposed joint physical custody, and she wanted sole physical custody, granting him reasonable and unlimited visitation. Before I could finish reading the proposal, he interrupted me, rose to his feet, and scowled down at his wife. She immediately dropped her head and fixed her eyes on her shoes as he barked, "This is a total waste of time. There will be no mediation. We will go to trial, and then you'll see what you get." Then, looking at me, he continued, "Put that in your official record, *Miss Counselor*, and tell the courts that I am through with this mediation bullshit. She thinks because she is finally getting her little divorce that she can have my kids too. Well, we'll see about that. The only way my kids stand a chance of achieving functional brains, and a successful future, is by living with me. Do you know who I am, *Miss Counselor*? Do you? I am one of the most well-respected litigation attorneys in this state. So…good luck to both of you." With that, he threw his papers on the floor and stormed out.

The woman cried into her hands. Although I felt like joining her, I swallowed the lump in my throat and began to inquire about what just happened. She said her husband was, in fact, a very well-known and successful lawyer, and that she would be doomed in trial because of his reputation and his connections. She said his intimidating style had snuffed out the courage—and flattened the egos—of many marriage counselors. No one could hold him accountable.

Her tone was despairing, and when I noticed, she said that she had been distraught for a very long time. Her husband was a difficult man and the product of a very painful childhood. She said that she loved him but just couldn't live with his scorching behaviors anymore, and no one seemed able to help. She was puzzled—how could someone so sweet and sensitive as a boy become such an overbearing egotist? We sighed together. I gave her some recommendations for support and the session ended. I turned in my noncompliance report, and that was the last I saw of them.

When I think about that couple, I wonder if anyone ever reached him, what happened to the children, what happened to her. I vividly remember my unease—my skin temperature rising, my heart rate increasing, my stomach knotting. A love of words, decent communication skills, and a chronic fascination with the human condition were silenced by an unfamiliar sensation, a loss of confidence. It wasn't just the bullying; it was his arrogant, entitled demeanor. It was as if he had stomped out my spunk and compromised my courage. This was the first of several similar sobering experiences in my early career. As my husband always says, "You don't know what you don't know." I had a lot to learn, especially about the complexities of narcissism vis-à-vis interpersonal relationships.

Pivotal Influences

I have immense curiosity about what makes people tick and a perpetual fascination with human behavior. The necessary decoding of my own emotional assembly is not exempt. Having spent a good deal of time trying to make sense of my own makeup, I've come to realize the value of ever-emerging personal discoveries.

Thirty years ago, I had the good fortune of meeting the incomparable Dr. Jeffrey Young, one of my mentors and dearest friends. He taught me how to integrate my philosophy of psychotherapy (then, cognitive therapy exclusively) within his richly textured schema therapy model—a superb approach for treating issues of narcissism. I am forever indebted to him for the profound impact he has had, and continues to have, on my life.

In 2003, I was granted another stroke of good luck when I met Dr. Daniel Siegel, the gifted master of interpersonal neurobiology. Under his supervision, I was able to attach an accessible and user-friendly understanding of the brain and memory activation to my work. My studies with Dan were tremendously invigorating and have inspired progress with some of my most difficult clients. Bringing in the science of the brain has strengthened the credibility and validity of the complex process of dealing with relationships in psychotherapy. It also helps mitigate the shame and stigma associated with seeking help for emotional problems; once clients understand how the brain holds experiences and how memory allows access to old painful events, they become less defensive about being labeled "crazy" or "weak." In addition, science removes some of the skepticism that many may feel entering therapy. It helps us appreciate the important workings of our fundamental biology and how this integrates with our life experiences.

Shared Wisdom

It has been many, many years since that painful meeting in the family mediation office. I have spent a lot of time struggling, experimenting, studying, and carving my niche. Ironically, I am now an expert in narcissism, having worked with this population and the "offended others" for years now. My clients are mostly narcissistic men, some narcissistic women, and people who are trying to cope with narcissists in their lives. I'm not sure how to explain this passion. My colleagues tend to find it a bit unusual, even masochistic, as most clinicians shudder at the thought of working with narcissists and many will not accept referrals of this type. For me, it is actually a very rewarding experience, both personally and professionally.

Not every narcissist is willing or able to do the transformational work, but some will—with leverage (high-stakes consequences), a sturdy therapist, and the right treatment approach (preferably one that dives deep into the emotional narrative). Therapists have also found this book an instrumental resource, even though intended to help those dealing with a narcissistic other.

Disarming the Narcissist will define and illustrate different types of narcissism, offer explanations for why and how narcissism develops as part of a person's personality, and provide guidance and tools for effectively surviving (even thriving) in relationships with these challenging folks. It will help you identify your own life patterns and themes so that you can understand why you may be drawn to narcissistic people, and how you might get triggered or stuck when dealing with them. It will help you develop a reflective and sturdy voice when communicating intentions, needs, and expectations with the narcissist in your life. This book is designed to assist you not only in getting through difficulties, but also in achieving improved and satisfying experiences when addressing a narcissist.

One thing to note is that most experts in the field propose that more than 75 percent of narcissists are male, and for this reason, I've used the male pronoun more often in this book. (I am also more accustomed to working with male narcissists.) This is partly attributed to gender-related qualities, and socialization around emotional vulnerability, aggression, competitiveness, limited attachment to others, dominance, and societal norms, particularly as they apply to nature versus nurture issues in child development. Women can be narcissistic too, but they tend to express these traits within the domains of personal appearance, vanity, the status of their children or household, and their value as caregivers. In addition, narcissistic women are inclined toward more covert manifestations of this syndrome. They are likely to show up as martyrs, complainers, and gratuitous victims. Of course, you will also meet the grand dames, the divas, and the corporate moguls, who look more like their male counterparts in their pushy and oppressive quest for control, status, and approval.

The similarity between male and female narcissists is that both have an insatiable need to be the center of attention, whether overtly or covertly. This will limit, or even eliminate, any expressed empathy or remorse. You may have heard the term "narcissistic injury." This refers to the dynamic wherein, for a narcissist, saying a simple "I'm sorry" is like saying, "I am the worst human being on Earth." For all their bravado, they are easily injured by criticism, others' disappointment, differing points of view, lack of notice or compliments, being ignored, and even their own mistakes. But you won't necessarily know they are feeling injured because they are masterful cover-up artists. Instead of appearing wounded, they will hurl the prickliest words at you, avoid you, or demand your applause for their wonderfulness. You may find yourself surrendering, offering an "I'm sorry" of your own to quell their unrelenting reactions and mend their tattered egos.

But it need not be this way. It is possible to maintain your composure and self-esteem when dealing with narcissistic people. The first step is to develop an understanding of narcissism and how it arises—the topic of chapter 1. This can help you appreciate that while they can be very hurtful, the narcissist's actions and inactions are not your fault. You can discover how enlisting empathy for the narcissist—a paradoxically powerful tool—can allow you to hold them accountable, bringing you peace of mind, and a more satisfying relationship, or helping you determine when it's time to go.

Framing the Situation:
Toward an Understanding of Narcissism

The mass of men lead lives of quiet desperation.

—Henry David Thoreau

"Wendy, why should I spend (waste) my time learning about the narcissist? Don't I spend enough time just trying to deal with him? How is this helpful to me? What about my pain? Am I supposed to feel sorry for him for his wounded life?" Many readers ask these important questions. Let me answer the last question first. No, cultivating an understanding of narcissism is not intended to make you feel sorry for them or let them off the hook. The understanding, ironically, helps you to liberate yourself and hold *them* accountable. Too many of those offended by the narcissist end up haunted by feelings of self-doubt, self-blame, and hopelessness. The narcissist is masterful at compromising your emotional wisdom, leaving you filled with angst and anger—and over time these two emotional postures can be wearying. The more you understand the makeup of a narcissist, the greater your chances for emancipation from self-doubt, self-blame, and powerlessness— and the greater the opportunity to protect yourself, recapture your voice, and embrace your weary and precious self.

The narcissist both appeals and appalls. He may look like a modern-day Sir Lancelot, replete with swaggering charm and the shining armor of our time: a handsome portfolio, dazzling acquisitions. Beware! This knight is a master of illusion. He can be downright menacing. You may fall prey to his seductive lures, but his arrogance, condescension, sense of entitlement, and lack of empathy are formidable and inevitably lead to frustration and chronically difficult long-term relationships.

She may be found decorated in the trendiest of glad rags, strutting through some corporate headquarters, monopolizing a Monday night parent-teacher meeting, or delegating duties at a local community event. She may resemble the woman on the cover of the latest domestic diva magazine, in a push-up bra showcasing the consumer's most highly recommended quick-and-easy floor mop. This gal does it all, and she'll be the first to let you know that: "Well, I don't mean to brag, but..." or "You think you have it bad, let me tell you what bad really looks like..." or "No other woman would put up with..."

She is the most extraordinary sufferer, the most virtuous victim. She has unmatched self-sacrifice: "No one could possibly give up what I've given up for the people in my life..." This forgoing of her needs gets exaggerated when people stoke her high-pitched selflessness and craving for approval, by offering an awe-filled "I don't know how you do it." Indeed, this lovely yet unabashed matron of martyrdom demands applause, while, like nails on a chalkboard, the forgery of her modesty and perfectly perky posture leave us squirming.

The Narcissist at a Glance

After nearly thirty years of working with narcissists, I've learned that there are few greater challenges in psychotherapy. This could be the client in therapy because a partner mustered up the courage to say, "Get help or get out." Or perhaps his boss gave him an ultimatum after countless complaints about his difficult attitude. Maybe he's losing momentum in his competitive career and is looking for an edge. Maybe it's a litigious matter and he believes counseling might look good in his file. Occasionally, narcissists reluctantly enter therapy because they are simply lonely, depressed, or anxious.

So, what do we call these people who unbalance you with their complexity and omnipotence? Though they may seem well-assembled and self-assured, sometimes with a saccharine wit, they can quickly reduce you to apprehension, tears, boredom, or disgust. We call these people "narcissists." (As mentioned in the introduction, I'll primarily use the male pronoun and male examples; however, at the end of this chapter, you'll find material on female narcissists. Any pronoun may apply when it comes to narcissism.)

exercise: Is the Difficult Person in Your Life a Narcissist?

Read through the items listed below and check off any that apply to the difficult person in your life. Only check off a trait if it is expressed excessively, meaning it occurs more often than not. (This exercise is also available for download at www.newharbinger.com/47704. See back of book for more information.)

_____ Self-absorbed (acts like everything is all about him or her)

_____ Entitled (makes the rules and breaks the rules)

_____ Demeaning (puts you down and bullies you)

_____ Demanding (demands whatever he or she wants)

_____ Distrustful (is suspicious of your motives when you're being nice to him or her)

_____ Perfectionistic (has rigidly high standards; things are done his or her way or no way)

_____ Snobbish (believes he or she is superior to you and others; gets bored easily)

_____ Approval seeking (craves constant praise and recognition)

_____ Unempathic (is uninterested in understanding your inner experience or unable to do so)

_____ Unremorseful (cannot offer a genuine apology)

_____ Compulsive (gets overly consumed with details and minutiae)

_____ Addictive (cannot let go of bad habits; uses them to self-soothe)

_____ Emotionally detached (steers clear of feelings)

If you checked at least ten of the traits, the difficult person in your life most likely meets the criteria for overt maladaptive narcissism, the most common and difficult form. This type of narcissist is in your face and unwieldy. I call it "overt maladaptive narcissism" to differentiate it from other forms of narcissism, such as covert maladaptive narcissism and milder forms of narcissism. The terms "overt" and "maladaptive" here mean an observable inability to adequately fit in, conform, or adjust to conditions in the environment or basic expectations within relationships. If the narcissist in your life is truly an overt maladaptive narcissist, don't despair. You already knew you had your hands full, just not what to call it or what to do about it. But you're getting closer. Read on.

If you've checked a lesser number of items on the list, you may be dealing with a challenging but less obstreperous narcissist. Narcissism appears along a spectrum, from healthy and benign narcissism at one end to moderate and then overt or covert maladaptive narcissism at the other. I'll define all of these different types in this chapter.

What Is a Narcissist?

The term "narcissism" hails from Greek mythology's tale of Narcissus, who was doomed to eternally fall in love with his own reflection as punishment for refusing to accept the love of Echo, a mountain nymph. Because Narcissus craved but could never possess the image he saw reflected, he simply pined and was eventually turned into a beautiful flower. The moral of this evocative myth is that true beauty blossoms when obsessive and excessive self-love expires.

There is a lot written on this subject. Sadly, much of the literature actually describes a sociopathic profile or antisocial personality disorder.

Sociopaths appear to be self-righteous, and therefore, may resemble someone with a narcissistic personality, but sociopaths are typically more aggressive and devious, deriving actual pleasure from producing pain, without a sense of right versus wrong. They sometimes lack what neuroscientists might call a neuro-moral architecture in the brain.

Narcissists will indeed hurt us, but the hurt is often inflicted to protect their pride, possessions, or ego, rather than to create pain. Narcissists are self-absorbed and preoccupied with achieving the perfect image (recognition, status, or being envied). They appear to have little or no capacity for listening, caring, or understanding the needs of others, which can leave them without true intimacy, the feeling of being understood and held safely and lovingly by another person. Such connections allow us to experience the difference between love of self and love of another. Learning how to balance self-directed with other-directed attention is an important part of childhood development. It is fundamental to the development of reciprocity, responsibility, and empathy. Unfortunately, it is usually lacking in the narcissist's early development.

The narcissist may sport a brash and boastful ego while unknowingly yearning, like all of us, for the safe refuge found within a heartfelt embrace. While he may seem to have little or no regard for your needs and feelings, only willing to garner your attention through entitlement and obnoxiousness, the truth is that he actually longs for a deeper and more profound connection, which he simply cannot comprehend, or accept. He's likely to view the idea of an emotionally intimate connection as weak and pathetic. His unmet emotional needs drive him to seek your attention through charming, oratorical, and unnerving behaviors.

Origins of Narcissism

Once upon a time, this braggart was simply a child with wants, needs, and feelings, like any other child. What led that child toward an expectation of center stage, a spotlight of specialness, and rules that do not apply to him? Let's take a look at a few possible explanations. Remember, this is not to have you feeling sorry for the narcissist, or to let him off the hook. This is to guide your understanding of how narcissists become who they are and to emancipate you from internalized self-doubt and self-blame.

The Spoiled Child

One theory is that a narcissist may have grown up in a home where being better than others and having special rights and privileges was critically important. In this home, few limits were set and no significant consequences were assigned for overstepping boundaries or breaking rules. His parents may not have adequately taught him how to manage or tolerate discomfort, perhaps utterly indulging him. This dynamic primed him for reenactments in adulthood and set the stage for the development of the *purely spoiled narcissist*.

The Dependent Child

Another proposal is that one or both parents hovered too close, making the child's life as discomfort-free as possible. Instead of teaching and encouraging the development of age-appropriate life skills, such as tolerating necessary frustrations, his parents may have done everything for him. As a result, he was robbed of a sense of personal competence and instead felt helpless and dependent. He may have grown up feeling entitled to have others take care of everything so he wouldn't face discomfort, humiliation, or feeling like a failure. We may also find this in cultures where males (sometimes females) are treated like "little princes" and given little responsibility or preparation for managing everyday tasks and frustrations.

The Lonely, Deprived Child

The most popular theory is one we often encounter in the treatment room. It's the story of a child who grew up feeling conditionally loved based on performance. His parents may have expected him to be the best, instilling that to be anything short of perfect is to be flawed, inadequate, and unlovable. He may have been taught that love is tentative and contingent, or that his emotional needs would be met if he achieved greatness. His parents may have sought pride and attention through his achievements, implying a less-than-perfect performance would devastate them.

This scenario may be complicated by different treatment from each parent. These children are often criticized by one parent while doted on, overprotected, or used as a surrogate spouse by the other. They may comply with their parents' demands and expectations to receive attention and dodge criticism and shame. In response to this profound emotional deprivation, manipulation, and stifling of the precious and vulnerable little self, the child develops an attitude of *I will need no one, No one is to be trusted, I will take care of myself,* or *I'll show you.*

He was not loved for being himself, and was neither guided nor encouraged in the discovery of his true inclinations. He was not made to feel completely safe and unquestionably cherished by a caregiver. He was not shown how to walk in someone else's shoes—how to feel the inner emotional life of another person. There was no role model for empathy and attunement. He was left with shame and a sense of defectiveness, both from the direct criticism and from the withholding of emotional nourishment and, often, physical affection. He was made to feel there was something wrong with him, as if wanting comfort, attention, and understanding were weaknesses. In defense, he mustered up whatever safeguards he could to extinguish the pain.

The Mixed Bag

You might find that "his majesty" and "her highness" are best described by a combination of the origins proposed above. Given the complexity of human interactions (and reactions), it's hardly surprising that people come by their character as a result of a combination of factors.

Spoiled-dependent. The narcissist in your life might have been both spoiled and dependent. In this case, not only will he act entitled and feel superior (not surprising given the family modeling of a "we're better than others" attitude), but he may also feel dependent and incompetent (from parents always waiting on him and rescuing him instead of helping him develop the necessary skills). As an adult, he may show up as entitled and expect to be indulged, or he may avoid taking initiative and making decisions because he has an underlying fear of exposing his limitations and a crisp inability to tolerate frustration.

Deprived-dependent. Another combination is being both deprived and dependent. In this case, he will be easily offended as well as dependent, needing others to constantly reassure him and manage life for him. Discreetly, he seeks out others to protect him from a deeply felt shame about his defective, lonely, and inadequate self. He may seem needy and hypersensitive, rather than demanding and show-offish. He may be addicted to self-soothing behaviors, such as working, spending, gambling, pornography, overeating, and so on. You might refer to him as a high-maintenance type. And while he may have a longer fuse, beware. When he's forced to face frustration or finds himself the butt of too many jousts in verbal repartee, his sensitivity may either launch him into tyrannical verbal assaults or cause him to disappear within his stonewalled, silent abyss. He may also lick his wounds with self-stimulating activities, such as cybersex, gambling, or even drugs.

While some experts speculate that the manifestations of narcissism stem from biologically determined personality traits, most feel a combination of early experiences and temperament are responsible. It's important to note that many children grow up in environments like those described above without becoming narcissistic. These children may have experienced a different outcome because of a more stable temperament—a loving grandparent, teacher, or caregiver who filled the void and helped instill healthy and adaptive disciplinary tools. It is usually the case that biology and environment work together to create personality and character.

exercise: What Type of Narcissist Are You Dealing With?

Think about the narcissist you're dealing with. On the list below, check off any tendencies that pertain to the narcissist. (Of course, if you know the person's childhood history, you may already have some helpful clues.) This exercise will help you identify the most popular forms of narcissism, especially the deprived type. However, there can be a great deal of variation. If your narcissist doesn't fit neatly into the categories below, he or she may be more purely the spoiled type or dependent type.

Spoiled-Dependent

_____ Speaks as if he or she is superior to others, whether in terms of looks, intelligence, accomplishments, or other regards. (Example: "After all, I *do* have an Ivy League education.")

_____ Expects special attention from almost everyone or acts as though the rules don't apply to him or her. (Example: "What do you mean, I have to *wait* to be seated?!")

_____ Interrupts others when they are speaking, assuming that his or her words are of much greater import. (Example: "No, no, the real issue is...")

_____ Prone to temper tantrums or avoidance when things don't go his or her way. (Example: "What do you mean you didn't make the reservations? I insisted on going to Cafe Grande!")

_____ Speaks in long-winded monologues and views himself or herself as an expert on everything. (Examples: "What I think is..." "My opinion is..." "So, as I've told you, blah, blah, blah.")

Deprived-Dependent

_____ Constantly fishing for compliments, recognition, and favors; feels insecure and inadequate underneath the appearance of a sturdy facade. (Examples: "So you really liked what I did, didn't you?" "Looks good on me, don't you think?")

_____ Demands explanations and clarification in conversations; often feels that people are trying to hurt, humiliate, or take advantage of him or her. (Examples: "What exactly are you saying about me?" "Are you calling me a liar?" "So now you think nothing I do is good enough?")

_____ Turns on you or hides when frustrated or hurt; feels entitled to protect his or her ego through attack, distraction, or consumption. (Examples: "How dare you!" "What can I expect, given your limitations?" "I'll show you.") Works excessively, overeats, gets consumed by projects that never get completed, compulsively surfs the internet, drinks too much, has affairs, spends excessive amounts of money.

_____ Denies, defends, and demeans you (usually in that order) when you discover a betraying behavior, such as sexual acting out, dangerous spending habits, legal infractions, gaslighting (distorting reality to save face or to have his or her way).

Review the items you marked and notice if your narcissist fits more into the spoiled-dependent category or the deprived-dependent one. If you find that he or she has all or almost all of the traits from both categories, this may indicate the lonely, deprived child. Such people tend to harbor the tendencies listed above and deploy them under conditions that may be reminiscent of their childhood experiences.

If your narcissist is the spoiled-dependent type, change will require more emphasis on setting limits and some lessons about tolerating frustration. For the deprived-dependent type, there will be a need to ignore boastful commentaries and instead pay attention to the narcissist's "ordinary" niceties and thoughtful gestures, when they appear. Such people will also need to be held accountable for angry outbursts and be encouraged to develop reflective self-regulating tools for calming overly reactive anger. Establishing collaborative exit strategies, such as time-outs, will also be helpful.

Of course, the causative factors and problematic behaviors will be unique to each individual, requiring a tailored approach. Later, I'll elaborate on these issues and change strategies, as well as other interventions for change.

The Magician: The Great Disappearing Act!

The narcissist is on a constant quest to win emotional autonomy, meaning that he only needs himself. His personal longings and hardships are typically concealed beneath a cloak of success, power, competitiveness, righteousness, or some combination thereof. He might be the glory seeker, the contester, or the perennial master of ceremonies. Perhaps he is always ready to rescue the damsel in distress, to persist in proving a point until you scream uncle, or to entertain you with name-dropping or clever storytelling. However, his emotional illiteracy, detachment, and withdrawal from emotional encounters, and his hyperautonomous stance, limits his capacity for empathy or precludes it all together.

When you are in an exchange with an empathic person, you feel the person truly gets you. Empathic people seem to understand your feelings and your experience, even if they have a different point of view. Empathy is the ability and willingness to imagine walking in the other person's shoes. Unlike sympathy, it is not simply feeling sorrow for another's pain; it is the art of tuning in to it, allowing it to resonate within yourself. It is one of the most powerfully connective qualities of a healthy relationship, and its absence can be devastating. Daniel Goleman, in his book *Social Intelligence* (2006), suggests that someone who doesn't empathize with others can treat them as objects rather than as people.

Now You See Him, Now You Don't

The narcissist's lack of empathy can manifest in different ways. For example, if you are able to wedge a word into a conversation, asking him to tune in to your world, he's likely to disappear like Houdini before your very eyes. He may literally walk away in the middle of your sentence, interrupt you, or announce an important "something" that he must get to right away.

And when life presents you with a crisis, the narcissist becomes more entrenched in his absence. Suddenly you find yourself needing to focus on yourself, perhaps fighting for your life or the life of a loved one, while the "inconvenienced one" becomes even more obnoxious, unhelpful, selfish, or checked out. When my dad was very ill and eventually dying, my self-sacrificing clients actually felt guilty coming in for their sessions, despite my repeated reassurance that I really wanted to be there for them. On the other hand, my narcissistic clients often seemed visibly annoyed if I arrived at a session a little late after a visit to the hospital, which reconfirmed the diagnosis of narcissism.

Hiding Behind the Armor of Coping Modes

The narcissist's reactions are swift and diverse. Perhaps he puts you down for your "silly" emotional needs when you make a request or voice a complaint. He may talk over you with an insistent (and avoidant) soliloquy on the differences between apples and oranges, wants and needs, Plato and Aristotle, Democrats and Republicans, or any number of other non sequiturs. A narcissist in a coping mode, even a self-aggrandizing one, is essentially hiding.

He may offer you a reply, such as, "I don't know what you want from me," then point out all the ways in which he is above reproach. Narcissists consistently hide their insecurities so that no one can hurt, humiliate, disappoint, or use them again. However, hiding behind false bravado means they forfeit the intimate joys and sorrows that are part of life's journey and, along with them, many of their own desires.

If you're in a romantic relationship with a narcissist, he may feel threatened by his vulnerability the minute you ask him for a tour of his inner emotional domain, or you invite him to wander through yours. Noteworthy: It's likely that what he actually feels is an *unrealized* fear of tuning in to his vulnerable side, experiencing himself as the defective, lonely, and shameful little pest he was engineered to believe he was. So, he'll push this part of himself out of his awareness in any way he can. In so doing, he pushes you away as well. This absence of emotional intimacy can leave you experiencing loneliness, even when the narcissist is right beside you.

A client said she found herself less lonely when her narcissistic husband traveled than when he was in the same room. She had no expectations when he was away, whereas when he was home, his inability to be emotionally available left her feeling even lonelier and more deprived. Her husband, she realized, was using an evasive strategy of deafening emotional silence. To him, any exposure of his vulnerability would feel like a fusing of the two of them in some needy and dependent way. This is unthinkable for the narcissist, whose mission is one of sovereign self-reliance.

Marion Solomon, PhD, writes in her early book *Narcissism and Intimacy* (1992) that the narcissist fears the loss of a sense of self when entering an emotional merger. For narcissists, intimacy feels like a stifling and dangerous dwelling.

The Mantras: His and Hers

"I will need no one" and *"You owe me"* are the resounding and self-affirming mantras of the narcissist. These are, of course, completely outside of the narcissist's awareness—a melody that plays repeatedly in the background, thanks to well-grooved memories. This intricate memory system is also the residence of the narcissist's maladaptive coping modes: well-worn masks.

The Masks

The narcissist's masks allow him to transform potential pain into a bearable, even comfortable, experience. Donning a mask is a way to handle uncomfortable, upsetting feelings. These masks might be viewed as a metaphor for protection, also known as a "coping mode."

Here are some of the most common modes, or masks, of the narcissist:

- The bully/controller

- The show-off/approval-seeker

- The addictive self-soother

- The entitled rule breaker

Chapter 5 provides a more detailed discussion of these masks and explains how to effectively deal with them. Other masks the narcissist might adopt are the workaholic, the superhero, and the morally self-righteous martyr. The strategies offered for the four most common masks can be adapted to deal with other masks that you might identify.

The Narcissist's Strategy for Dealing with Unmet Needs

Based on their memories of unmet childhood needs, many narcissists believe their needs will never be met. This fear is at the root of the narcissist's flimsy and superficial attachments to others. He compensates for the fear of not having his needs met through an excessively autonomous style. The fear and overcompensation lead to a lack of intimacy with himself, a void of *self-knowing*.

When a narcissist tries to escape difficult feelings, he may automatically shift into one of the coping modes listed above, donning whatever mask he needs. These maladaptive coping modes become the characteristically negative behaviors you may see. Unfortunately, these masks perpetuate the feelings he seeks to avoid, re-creating the all-too-familiar shame, loneliness, mistrust, and deprivation of early experiences. For example, to avoid awkwardness in a social setting, he will complain of being bored or launch into a grandstanding monologue. Consequentially, he will appear not only awkward, but rude and obnoxious as well.

Jeffrey Young, founder of schema therapy (which we'll explore in chapter 2) and an expert on narcissism, writes about the high costs of hiding one's true self: loss of joy, spontaneity, trust, and intimacy (Young and Klosko 1994). He describes how the narcissist may look fine on the surface, but underneath he feels defective and unloved.

Covert Narcissism

Now and then, narcissists show up camouflaged in quiet nobility. These morally self-righteous martyrs are forever pointing out the "right" and "wrong" way of living. They differentiate themselves from "prejudiced," "selfish," or "lazy" people. Quick to the rescue, covert narcissists are eager to find solutions to your problems. They will spout their philosophy with lots of "should" and "must," "always" and "never," and "all or nothing." They'll proclaim the world would be a better place if people just paid attention and followed the rules—their rules, of course!

The covert narcissist proudly declares an allegiance to the truth. He offers his humbleness and human imperfection to impress you. Behind this thin veil, he modestly confesses his loyalty to rigorous self-improvement. He might say, "Sure, I could talk about the ten-thousand-dollar donation I made to the humanitarian foundation, but I don't need praise for my philanthropy."

The covert narcissist can hide behind a facade of morally upstanding servitude for a while, but just wait. Like all narcissists, he hungers for recognition, so he will be captured by the throbbing pain of the deprived and lonely child within, longing to be noticed. He will reveal his ravenous appetite for recognition as an extraordinary human being—not an ordinary terrestrial, but something more akin to an archangel. With little tolerance for his basic needs and little confidence in achieving love and connection, the narcissist reaches for grand recognition and approval to affirm his emotional independence.

It is particularly difficult for him to escape the pain he feels when the honors received aren't spectacular enough or the spotlight fades too quickly. In time, resentment and frustration jiggles the tightrope of his seemingly tidy and stoic disposition and down he falls, landing upon whomever happens to be in his path. You may find yourself the subject of his cold eyes, upturned nose, and clenched brow. You may be treated to an artful diatribe on the ungrateful and imbecilic nature of people and bureaucracies. He spews because he is disappointed at receiving less than a five-minute standing ovation and counterattacks with smug gestures or lambasting commentaries, and through this tantrum he hoists himself back up on his self-righteous throne.

Covert narcissists can also show up in subtler (passive-aggressive) forms. They will "act out" by arriving late to the appointment they did not want to attend. They will cancel a meeting at the last minute to assert their authority. They will avoid decision-making or collaborative planning, as in vacation plans, until they wear you down with frustration, and ultimately make a unilateral decision or no decision at all.

The Difference Between Male and Female Narcissists

Male and female narcissists share many traits. Both can be identified by their love of their own voice and ceaseless search for approval and admiration. Both will assault you with their opinions, complaints, and criticisms until your very last nerve is frayed or you are bored to tears. If you try to wedge a word in during their monologue, you'll suddenly become invisible. They only have ears for the rising crescendo of their lofty vocals or your admiration. What they see in that shiny, glazed-over look on your face is their own reflection, not your exasperated boredom. Because they have yet to develop the capacity for empathy, they don't understand that their efforts to impress you are actually flooding you with fantasies of an emergency exit.

Because the majority of narcissists are male, the examples throughout this book tend to focus on how narcissism manifests in men. However, 30 percent of the narcissist types examined in this book are female, and they tend to have similar as well as different characteristics. So, let's take a look at what distinguishes these divas, drama queens, grand dames, prima donnas, femme fatales, and matrons of martyrdom from their male counterparts.

"Narcissisters": The Lowdown on Her Highness

The female narcissist may be a temptress who beseeches you with saucy sauntering, or withers you with self-effacing sanctimony. A particularly common type of female narcissist is the victim or martyr: She might capture you with her exasperated "I'm everything to everyone" and perceived lack of appreciation. This virtuous victim is seldom more than half a breath away from her next emotive purge. Should you mention that you aren't feeling well or that you're running late for an appointment, your needs will vanish within the gravity of her immense self-importance.

Mired in martyrdom, if you dare to disagree with or ignore her, she'll make you pay by pouting, sobbing, or maybe even threatening to abandon you or hurt herself. It can feel like you've been granted the supporting actor role in a low-budget movie: She might drop to the couch, clutching her chest and complaining of a sharp pain. Reduced to fear, you may offer a groveling apology and promise to attend to her more closely. You may recant your opinions and agree with her, or offer excuses. You may even praise her for her graciousness and thank her for giving you a second chance.

If you haven't dealt with this type of narcissist, this story may sound like a melodrama. But it's exactly the scene described to me by Bob, a client who contacted me about his narcissistic bride-to-be. He was so alarmed by her chest pains that he called 911 because he thought she was having a heart attack—much to the shock and embarrassment of his fiancée.

The "narcissister" will have your mind bending like a contortionist. Should you fight her fiery theatrics, she will shift into a pageantry of sniffles and sassy smugness. Yes, she has your number on speed dial: self-doubt, guilt, and rejection. And this narcissister will get you to answer her call every time.

Narcissistic Mothers

When the queen in question is your mother, it ups the ante. One client shared that she and her mother were once at an outdoor concert when her mom looked at her, shielding her eyes, and said, "Change seats with me, Deborah. The sun is in my eyes." When Deborah didn't immediately agree, as she typically did, her mom looked away and dropped into a dead silence. It may sound like a small incident, but it was just one in a lifetime of similar instances where the ice queen put her own needs before those of her child.

Growing up with a narcissistic parent can be a strong predictor for the development of narcissistic traits. So, how was Deb spared from developing a narcissistic personality herself? As stated earlier, temperament, mood, emotional and behavioral inclinations, and environmental influences are all factors in shaping the personality of the child. As a young girl, Deb was inhibited and anxious, startled easily, and often felt guilty when her mom was upset. Often children of narcissistic parents are indoctrinated with the belief that it's their job to make the parent happy and their fault when the parent is upset.

Deb had a natural response to her mom's repeated distress siren: "You should be ashamed of yourself, young lady. Don't you dare embarrass me! You are an ingrate! After all I've done for you… You're such a disappointment. What a bad mother I must be [whimper, pout, sniffle]." In addition, Deb's father was extremely self-sacrificing and intimidated by his wife. In the service of peace, he always agreed with or gave in to his wife. It's no wonder that Deb picked up what he modeled, considering her limited power and desire for stability, safety, love, and acceptance.

Vanity Thy Name Is…

Narcissistic women tend to place much importance on their physical appearance, flaunting their bodily attributes and augmentations. "Mirror, mirror on the wall…" is the mantra of the femme fatale. Female narcissists tend to place emphasis on a high fashion IQ, trendy decor, and meticulously accessorized children. In our social media age, this might be simply competitive socialization gone awry. Narcissistic women, much like their male counterparts, however, are wildly concerned with the opinions of those with perceived special value based on title, reputation, power, or incomparable good looks.

Blogger Susan Walsh (2010) makes some interesting observations about this phenomenon: "During the 70s and 80s, Americans became obsessed with celebrity culture, and eating disorders skyrocketed. Today, social media breeds narcissism by constantly encouraging women to post flattering photos and create online profiles that stress their uniqueness. [Social media sites] require self-promotion, bringing out the narcissist in us." Female narcissists might fantasize about their lives being viewed as a blockbuster hit, or a *Kardashianesque* series, where they are the enviable bombshell, receiving adulation at all times.

In an era of young girls clad in pink "Princess" T-shirts, a worrisome message emerges. This worry is backed up by surveys of college students and young adults that indicate a culture of specialness and entitlement. It seems that more and more young women (and men) are adopting a disturbing ideology of self-government that I refer to as a narcisstocracy. Under this self-serving administration, they come to believe that the only things that matter in life are looking great, excelling in performance, and winning the attention of important people. If they do these things, they believe the world will come to their door. They aren't concerned about the needs of others or the impact of their behavior unless it gets in the way of what they want. Most importantly, this growing breed is marinated in a saucy blend of sugary specialness, spicy entitlement, and second-to-none suffering for any frustration large or small.

Healthy Narcissism

Narcissism sounds like a disaster, doesn't it? But is narcissism always bad? Actually, no. Healthy narcissism contains assertiveness and self-respect. While "healthy narcissism" sounds like an oxymoron, narcissism actually occurs along a spectrum. Embodied in human nature itself is a tendency for narcissistic expression. And that isn't all bad.

Healthy Childhood Narcissism

Nearly every child comes into the world with the capacity to be impulsive, angry, and demanding (as well as joyful, playful, and curious). These qualities are simply elements of the broad spectrum of emotions linked to a child's natural vulnerability and innate temperament. Narcissism has robust value for children. It helps them express their physical and emotional discomfort, especially in the preverbal years. The child becomes angry, cries, and demands attention to obtain protection, approval, comfort, and playful engagement. This is healthy and developmentally appropriate behavior.

A wise and loving approach to parenting seeks to provide the emotional and physical support that will allow the child to become secure and competent. It works to provide reasonable limits and foster a healthy balance between receptivity to others and self-directed attention. Most parents hope their children will grow up with a healthy sense of entitlement, meaning they will maintain their sense of self-worth and know they deserve to be respected and included. Parents also want their children to respect the rights of others. And they must instill all of this despite the unsolved mysteries of parenting, their own lingering issues, and their child's unique temperament. This can be a daunting task for any parent.

In *Parenting from the Inside Out* (Siegel and Hartzell 2004), Daniel Siegel writes about the need for parents to make sense of their own early life experiences and to create healthy and coherent personal narratives so they can raise children who will thrive. Parents who learn how to connect the dots of their own journey have a heightened chance of offering loving and skillful discipline to their children.

In a loving and grounded parent-child relationship, shame can play an appropriate role in discipline as a means of calibrating the barometer of give-and-take and teaching family values and personal responsibility. With this approach, the child learns how to be accountable without feeling flawed and damaged. The goal is to foster celebration of her creativity and self while also developing a sense of responsibility to others. As the late gifted poet and philosopher John O'Donohue said, "A home is a place where a set of different destinies begin to articulate and define themselves. It is the cradle of one's future" (2000, 31).

In summary, healthy childhood narcissism evolves into integrity— the art of making a promise and keeping it. It harnesses an authentic picture of the child, not a cloaked one. It enables the child to articulate her intentions, needs, and purpose in the world with clarity and sensitivity to others. Healthy narcissism allows for a sturdier and more secure attachment to others, promoting sentiments of responsibility and reciprocity.

Healthy Adult Narcissism

The phrase "healthy adult narcissism" may describe a particular person who has achieved a degree of recognition and who is currently making a difference in the community or in the world. This person may also have had a profoundly personal impact on your life. People who exhibit healthy adult narcissism may or may not have had wise and loving parenting or a stable and healthy home. Their beginnings may have been stormy and turbulent. They may have come by this "healthy" evolution through therapy, spiritual guidance, or any number of self-help practices. They may be innately prone to caring for others, or have experienced the healing kindness of a teacher, a friend, a mentor, or a lover.

While success and celebrity are often features of odious and challenging people with overt maladaptive narcissism, many successful people inhabit the domain of well-adjusted, or healthy, narcissism. Why do we still use the term "narcissism" with this group? In part because those who often possess above-average dexterity and prowess aren't the "nice guy" when it comes to persistence and dealing with opponents.

Oprah Winfrey, for example, like other icons of the media, makes us feel grateful for healthy adult narcissism. Without it, the eye-opening issues and lessons of transformation that emerge from her provocative interviews might not reach us. Through keen, frank, and sometimes prickly confrontations, viewers and readers come to witness missions of hope, humility, and possibility and develop a profound connection to personal responsibility.

So how might we characterize healthy adult narcissists? Typically, they possess many of the following traits and express them with intensity:

Persistent: They will push their agenda until they get what they want, but mainly for the benefit of others.

Empathic: They are capable of strong attunement to the inner world of others.

Engaging: They are charismatic, socially literate, and interpersonally companionable, but they don't suffer fools.

Leadership: They can conceptualize a purpose or a vision and can formulate a direction when collaborating with others, while retaining their values.

Self-possessed: They are highly confident and rigorously committed to their missions. They are generous, dedicated, and unafraid of being real.

Recognition seeking: They are fueled by positive approval, but not dependent on it as in pathologic narcissism, while motivated to make a difference.

Determined: They can push beyond dense briars of opposition.

Confrontational: They don't flinch when it comes to holding others accountable, but they do this without assassinating one's soul.

Wisely fearful: They can discern between reasonably disquieting solicitation and destructive seduction.

Unapologetic: They are unapologetic for their confident determination and keeping-an-eye-on-the-ball maneuvers, even when (though unintended) other's feelings may get hurt along the way.

Conclusion

In this chapter, you've learned about the various types of narcissism, the most typical and oppressive being overt maladaptive narcissism. You've learned about the origins and impacts of narcissists. You've seen how narcissism manifests, how it might differ by gender, and a glimpse of the possibility for change and transformation. As you'll see, change is hard but, under certain conditions, it is possible. It requires innovative, courageous, and careful execution. There is a conspiracy of silence between the narcissist and his authentic self, between you and your most authentic feelings when you're in his company, and between the two of you in your interactions.

Chapter 2 will look at theories in psychotherapy that shed light on narcissism and begin to explore how these theories can be integrated into a workable approach to the challenging emotional labyrinth we all confront when dealing with the narcissist. Remember, knowledge equals liberation from self-doubt and self-blame.

CHAPTER 2

Understanding the Anatomy of Personality: *Schemas and the Brain*

History, despite its wrenching pain, cannot be unlived, but if faced with courage, need not be lived again.

—Maya Angelou

In addition to personal curiosity, years of professional experience, and exposure to many talented minds in the field, three leading experts have influenced my work: Aaron Beck, developer of cognitive therapy; Jeffrey Young, creator of schema therapy; and Daniel Siegel, a trailblazer in interpersonal neurobiology. Their work can illuminate how you deal with the narcissist in your life. In this chapter, I'll use insights from these experts to look at the notion of life themes, living at the mercy of our memories, and the power of natural inclinations. While still working to understand the narcissist, I'll encourage you to think about your own stories and notice how the matrix of the mind and the biology of the brain can present fierce challenges. This background will help you understand what is required for growth and change in your relationship with a narcissist.

Cognitive Therapy

Aaron Beck, known as the father of cognitive therapy, has given countless people a compass for navigating the complex terrain of our mental and emotional belief systems. His work is internationally recognized, and his approach has been proven highly effective in helping people change dysfunctional patterns. For example, as the narcissist learns to examine and accurately rescript his story and biased assumptions, he is freed from the long-standing patterns of behavior that lead to his bothersome coping behaviors, which *you* end up facing.

Cognitive therapy calls for an examination of the meanings we attach to people, places, and things. It is a well-woven tapestry of concepts and strategies for correcting the biased assumptions we often connect to our negative emotional experiences and self-defeating behavior. For the narcissist, cognitive therapists facilitate a collaborative process by which the narcissist develops more accurate ideas, beliefs, and predictions, to replace the distorted thoughts that have been embedded in his mind. Emphasis is placed on self-talk and testing the reality of inner dialogues. Beck's model has provided fertile ground for the growth of other forms of therapy, particularly schema therapy.

Schema Therapy

Schema therapy is an integrative model of psychotherapy founded by Jeffrey Young that combines proven cognitive and behavioral techniques with other widely practiced therapies. Young's approach is accessible to the general public in books such as *Reinventing Your Life* (Young and Klosko 1994), and to professionals in books such as *Schema Therapy: A Practitioner's Guide* (Young, Klosko, and Weishaar 2006). Studies show that schema therapy offers remarkable results for difficult clients (e.g., Giesen-Bloo et al. 2006, and many more) and is an effective treatment for dealing with issues of narcissism.

Understanding Schemas

Young's schema therapy proposes eighteen early maladaptive schemas that show up in adulthood as dysfunctional life themes (also called "buttons" or "life traps"). They are considered *early* maladaptive schemas because they derive from childhood and adolescent experiences where fundamental needs are not adequately met, which interferes with healthy and stable development. Schemas are beliefs or cognitions, involving emotional and bodily sensations, along with biological elements such as temperament.

Temperament refers to the innate character of the child. Children exhibit certain natural inclinations, such as shyness, aggression, extroversion, introversion, sensitivity, adaptability, buoyancy, and so on, which are shaped by genetic makeup and are observable in early phases of a child's development. For example, some children will avoid novel experiences or strangers and cling to their caregiver or a familiar object.

Personality emerges from the interplay of the child's temperament and the environment, which can modify natural inclinations. For example, if a shy child is scorned and humiliated by a parent or caregiver, she might develop an exacerbated tendency to withdraw and become depressed, or paradoxically, she might retaliate with aggressive noncompliance or passive avoidance and detachment. A child in this situation could develop a negative self-appraisal, also known as a defectiveness schema, wherein she feels flawed because she's shy.

On the other hand, if a parent of a shy child shows patience and acceptance, guiding her gently to take small steps beyond her comfort zone, the child could develop confidence in certain novel and social situations. In this scenario, self-acceptance is possible. It is true that temperament can change. It isn't altogether clear what predicts lifelong versus transient temperament, but we know that schemas result from the interplay between a child's temperament and the difficulties she confronts in her environment.

Schemas may be dormant for much of one's life, only becoming activated by conditions that either mimic or challenge the unyielding beliefs embodied within them. These "truths," which are the abiding content of the schema, have long been held and are difficult to refute. They are often connected with painful childhood memories, discreetly sheltered within the brain, and are experienced as visceral, meaning they are sensed (but not always sensible). Because they emerge outside of awareness and therefore aren't based on the present, the profound and often exaggerated resonance of schemas frequently leads to self-defeating behavior patterns.

When schemas are activated, the effects are similar to triggering traumatic or distressing memories. The emotional and physical circuits of the brain (subcortical regions) often disconnect from the executive, or decision-making, areas of the brain (cortical regions), which are responsible for distinguishing the "here and now" from the "there and then." When schemas are triggered, the release of stress hormones short-circuits the executive areas of the brain. If you're operating from "there and then," your reactions and decision-making can be influenced by events and emotions of the past rather than the present. And worst of all, you don't even realize it because it happens behind the scenes, outside of your awareness.

For example, if you have a schema of abandonment due to the inextinguishably painful memory of your father's disappearance when you were six years old, you may be especially sensitive to the thought of people leaving you. When your husband says he will be traveling on business, you feel that insecure knot in your belly and make unreasonable demands for contact and reassurance. This sets the stage for a relationship fraught with erosive issues of mistrust and dissatisfaction.

We all have schemas, typically more than one, formed in response to naturally imperfect and sometimes traumatic early life experiences. In many cases, noxious events such as abuse, neglect, abandonment, chaos, or excessive control cause schemas to fasten to a child's emotional makeup. This, in combination with biological predisposition, or temperament, ultimately sculpts our personality. When schemas are triggered ("He really pushed my buttons"), we may become flooded with uncomfortable physical sensations and biased thoughts and engage in self-defeating behaviors.

The Eighteen Early Maladaptive Schemas

In this chapter, you'll engage in a parallel process of discovery, looking at your schemas in conjunction with those of the narcissist. To begin, let's examine the eighteen early maladaptive schemas identified by Jeffrey Young. As you read, see if you can identify the schemas that feel true for you and keep an eye out for schemas that may hold sway over the narcissist in your life. Keep in mind that a schema is an emotional belief, first formed in your childhood or adolescence, that carries an exaggerated realness and intensity under certain conditions, even if it's dormant most of the time. (The material below is used with the kind permission of Jeffrey Young, PhD.)

1. Abandonment/instability. The perceived instability or unreliability of significant others. The sense that they will not be able to provide emotional support, connection, strength, or practical protection because they are emotionally unstable and unpredictable (for example, prone to angry outbursts), unreliable, or erratically present; because they will die imminently; or because they will abandon you in favor of someone better.

2. Mistrust/abuse. The expectation that others will hurt, abuse, humili-ate, cheat, lie, manipulate, or take advantage. Usually the harm is per-ceived as intentional or the result of extreme negligence. May include feeling always cheated or getting the short end of the stick.

3. Emotional deprivation. The expectation that others will not ade-quately meet your desire for normal emotional support. The major forms of deprivation are:

A.   **Deprivation of nurturance:** absence of attention, affection, warmth, or companionship

B.   **Deprivation of empathy:** absence of understanding, listening, self-disclosure, or mutual sharing of feelings

C.   **Deprivation of protection:** absence of strength, direction, or guidance

4. Defectiveness/shame. The feeling that you are defective, bad, unwanted, inferior, invalid, or unlovable if exposed. May involve hyper-sensitivity to criticism, rejection, and blame; self-consciousness, compari-sons, and insecurity around others; or shame regarding your perceived flaws. These flaws may be private (for example, selfishness, angry impulses, or unacceptable sexual desires) or public (such as undesirable physical appearance or social awkwardness).

5. Social isolation/alienation. The feeling that you are isolated from the rest of the world, different from other people, and/or not part of any group or community.

6. Dependence/incompetence. The belief that you are unable to handle everyday responsibilities in a competent manner without considerable help from others (for example, take care of yourself, solve daily problems, exercise good judgment, tackle new tasks, or make good decisions). Often feels like helplessness.

7. Vulnerability to harm or illness. Exaggerated fear of imminent and unpreventable catastrophe. Fears focus on one or more of the following: medical catastrophes or illnesses; emotional catastrophes, such as "going crazy"; or external catastrophes, such as elevators collapsing, criminal attack, airplane crashes, or earthquakes.

8. Enmeshment/undeveloped self. Excessive emotional involvement and closeness with one or more significant others (often parents) at the expense of individual identity or normal social development. You may believe you cannot survive or be happy without the constant support of the enmeshed other. You may feel smothered by or fused with others, a lack of sufficient individual identity, emptiness or without direction, or, in extreme cases, question your existence.

9. Failure. The belief that you have failed, will inevitably fail, or are fundamentally inadequate in areas of achievement (such as school, career, or sports). Often involves beliefs that you are stupid, inept, untalented, ignorant, lower in status, less successful than others, and so on.

10. Entitlement/grandiosity. The belief that you are superior to others, entitled to special privileges, or not bound by normal social rules. Often involves insistence that you should be able to do or have whatever you want, regardless of what is realistic or reasonable, or regardless of the cost to others. An exaggerated focus on superiority (for example, being the most successful, famous, wealthy) to achieve power or control (not primarily attention or approval) is common. Sometimes includes excessive competitiveness or domination of others: asserting power, forcing a point of view, or controlling the behavior of others without empathy.

11. Insufficient self-control/self-discipline. Difficulty or refusal to exercise sufficient self-control and tolerate frustration to achieve goals or restrain excessive emotions and impulses. In its milder form, you may tend to avoid discomfort—pain, conflict, confrontation, responsibility, or overexertion—at the expense of personal fulfillment, commitment, or integrity.

12. Subjugation. Excessive surrendering of control to others—usually to avoid anger, retaliation, or abandonment. The major forms of subjugation are:

> **A.   Subjugation of needs:** suppression of your preferences, decisions, and desires

> **B.   Subjugation of emotions:** suppression of emotional expression, especially anger

Usually involves the perception that your desires, opinions, and feelings are not valid or important to others, and a tendency toward excessive compliance combined with hypersensitivity to feeling trapped. Generally leads to anger, which can lead to passive-aggressive behavior, outbursts of temper, psychosomatic symptoms, withdrawal of affection, and substance abuse.

13. Self-sacrifice. Excessive focus on meeting the needs of others at the expense of your own gratification, most commonly to prevent causing others pain, avoid feeling selfish, or maintain a connection with others. Often results from an acute sensitivity to the pain of others. Sometimes leads to resentment and feeling your own needs are not being adequately met. (Overlaps with the concept of codependency.)

14. Approval seeking/recognition seeking. Excessive emphasis on gaining approval, recognition, fitting in, or attention from others, at the expense of developing a secure and true sense of self. Your self-esteem is dependent primarily on the reactions of others rather than yourself. Sometimes includes an overemphasis on status, appearance, social acceptance, money, or achievement—as means of gaining approval, admiration, or attention (not primarily power or control). Frequently results in hypersensitivity to rejection or unsatisfying and inauthentic major life decisions.

15. Negativity/pessimism. A pervasive, lifelong focus on the negative aspects of life (pain, death, loss, disappointment, conflict, guilt, resentment, unsolved problems, potential mistakes, betrayal, worry, and so on) while minimizing the positive. Usually includes exaggerated expectations—in a wide range of situations—that things will eventually go seriously wrong or will ultimately fall apart, even if they seem to be going well. Usually involves an inordinate fear of making mistakes that might lead to financial collapse, loss, humiliation, or being trapped in a bad situation. Because potential negative outcomes are exaggerated, chronic worry, vigilance, complaining, or indecision are common.

16. Emotional inhibition. The excessive inhibition of spontaneous action, feeling, or communication—usually to avoid disapproval by others, feelings of shame, or loss of control. The most common areas of inhibition involve anger and aggression; positive impulses (such as joy, affection, sexual excitement, or play); difficulty expressing vulnerability or communicating freely about your feelings, needs, and so on; and excessive emphasis on reason over emotion.

17. Unrelenting standards/hypercriticalness. The belief that you must strive to meet very high internalized standards of behavior and performance, usually to avoid criticism. Typically results in feelings of pressure or difficulty slowing down, and in hypercriticalness toward yourself and others. Involves significant impairment in pleasure, relaxation, health, self-esteem, sense of accomplishment, or satisfying relationships. Forms of unrelenting standards typically appear as:

A.   Perfectionism, inordinate attention to detail, or an underestimate of your performance relative to the norm

B.   Rigid rules and "shoulds" in many areas of life, including unrealistically high moral, ethical, cultural, or religious precepts

C.   Preoccupation with time and efficiency, so that more can be accomplished

18. Punitiveness. The belief that people should be harshly punished for making mistakes. Involves the tendency to be angry, intolerant, punitive, and impatient with people (including yourself) who do not meet your expectations or standards. Usually includes difficulty forgiving mistakes in yourself or others because of a reluctance to consider extenuating circumstances, allow for human imperfection, or empathize.

Jeffrey Young, PhD. Unauthorized reproduction without the written consent of the author is prohibited.

Using Schemas to Understand Interactions with a Narcissist

You might find that you and the narcissist in your life have, within your collections, some matching schemas, which may have originated from either similar or very different backgrounds. What differentiates the two of you is the way in which you cope with them. Let's say, for example, that you grew up with a mom who was very subjugated and self-sacrificing—not just giving and generous, but truly with little capacity to express her own needs and wants. Perhaps a "path of least resistance" person, she avoided confrontations and felt guilty for receiving attention. She may have occasionally shown signs of resentment when she was tired, overburdened, or felt stifled. You may have adopted this schema from witnessing her with people, including unruly ones. As a result, you may enact your self-sacrificing and subjugation schemas by giving in whenever the narcissist in your life activates the "play" button on your internal tape. This type of response is particularly characteristic of women.

Unfortunately, this coping style will perpetuate the very schemas you seek to escape. The more you give in to your self-sacrificing and subjugation beliefs—enabling the narcissist's bad habits—the more power they will have to keep you stuck. It's not your fault. It's automatic; and without awareness, understanding, and hard work, it will continue to show up like the sunrise each day.

The following list of schemas typically triggered by interactions with a narcissist will help you see that when you surrender as a means of coping, you actually block effective healing.

Typical Schemas That Get Triggered by Narcissists

- **Self-sacrifice:** It's tough to ask for what you need without feeling unworthy or guilty. Narcissists make it even tougher. You can get torn between feelings of guilt and resentment.

- **Subjugation:** It's difficult to assert your personal rights and opinions. Narcissists can be intimidating, forcing you to bury your anger or denying you your point of view.

- **Abandonment/instability:** Because you are so fearful of being rejected or alone, you will put up with the limitations and tormenting behaviors of your narcissist.

- **Defectiveness/shame:** Because you feel inadequate and undesirable, you easily buy into the criticisms that are hurled at you by the narcissist, taking the blame and feeling it's your fault when he's unhappy with you. You often feel that you need to fix yourself.

- **Emotional inhibition:** You are in the habit of keeping your feelings to yourself and are stoic and overly controlled when it comes to your emotions. The narcissist can have emotional outbursts, while you stand by in silent, invisible sorrow.

- **Emotional deprivation:** You don't believe you will find someone to meet your emotional needs, and to really love, understand, protect, and care about you. The narcissist lives up to your expectations. You are sad, but this is familiar.

- **Mistrust/abuse:** When he's hurtful, your relationship with the narcissist feels like a reenactment of the past. You know how to put up with it, and it feels impossible to fight. Even when you try to fight, you usually end up giving in.

- **Unrelenting standards:** You try harder and harder to be the perfect partner, friend, sibling, or employee, because you believe that this is expected of you. You compromise pleasure and spontaneity in an effort to live up to the narcissist's standards.

Now, as you read the following list of schemas typical of narcissists, note how he tries to fight his schemas or overcompensate for them. He avoids contacting the associated emotions and instead surrenders to them.

Typical Schemas Associated with Narcissism

- **Emotional deprivation:** No one will ever meet his needs and love him for who he is. Therefore, he must never need anyone. He strives for perfection, success, and autonomy.

- **Mistrust/abuse:** He believes that people are nice to him only because they want something from him. He avoids true intimacy and is highly skeptical of the motives of others.

- **Defectiveness/shame:** At his core, he feels unlovable and ashamed—feelings kept from his consciousness by addictive self-soothing activities (including workaholism), demanding approval for his outstanding performance, and acting entitled to special treatment.

- **Subjugation:** Control or be controlled. He is controlling.

- **Unrelenting standards:** There's no time for spontaneity, which can be a threat to his well-masked sense of inadequacy. He sacrifices pleasure for perfection, and often relentlessly. He's restless when not in performance mode.

- **Entitlement/grandiosity:** This is the narcissist's hallmark schema. He feels special when he's treated differently than others. Rules don't apply to him, and his grandiose dreams and supreme self-importance cover up a sense of defectiveness.

- **Insufficient self-control:** He refuses to accept limits and has little tolerance for discomfort. He wants what he wants, when and how he wants it. He cannot tolerate having to wait or being refused.

- **Approval seeking:** He constantly searches for recognition, status, and attention. This is usually overcompensation for his loneliness and sense of defectiveness.

Origins of the Narcissist's Schemas

Schemas correlated with the narcissist frequently arise in a scenario like this: Picture a child who was routinely criticized and devalued growing up. He was made to feel unworthy of love and attention, and ultimately, developed a defectiveness/shame schema. He also contracted the emotional deprivation schema because his caregivers didn't show him affection, understanding, or protection. His mistrust and subjugation schemas came from feeling controlled and manipulated by parents who built *their* self-esteem on his achievements and demanded he surrender his childhood needs. With no significant adult to counterbalance this experience and no repair work done by his depriving, critical parents, he grew up with loneliness, shame, and a well-entrenched feeling that no one would ever meet his emotional needs and that he was unlovable and flawed. These are the endlessly repeated lyrics of his schema, the biased beliefs that he has rigidly internalized.

The repetitive and painful feelings soon became file folders within his brain harboring the intractable "truths" that will define him, his future, and the world around him. His schemas acted as a blueprint for his emotional architecture. By early adulthood, simply entering a room full of strangers becomes a schema-triggering experience; he opens up the file folder and, based on the information within, anticipates being judged, ignored, or rejected.

As a child, he sought to escape the pain with coping skills that disabled healthy interpersonal connectedness but enabled him to thrive amid the voids and ruptures. Those coping skills often involve these protective masks:

- **The perfectionist:** the hallmark of an unrelenting standards schema

- **The avenging bully:** the hallmark of an entitlement schema

- **The competitive braggart:** the hallmark of an approval-seeking schema

Coping Responses in Schema Theory

Our human brains are wired to respond to a threat of danger with the fight-flight-freeze response system. You can fight back, run from or avoid the danger, or you can freeze, meaning give in or surrender. When a schema is triggered, it can feel threatening because the negative emotions, thoughts, physical sensations, and self-defeating reactions that arise out of early maladaptive experiences are extremely powerful. Circumstances that mirror the memories will send a message to the brain, which responds to the perceived threat by attempting to fight, flee, or surrender to the schema. All three responses are mechanisms for keeping the schema from getting its mighty grip on us—weapons for battle with the internal phantom. As explained above, typically when schemas are triggered, you are not aware of what is really happening, only of the feeling of danger or imminent threat based on a suggestive stimulus.

For example, let's say your supervisor walks by you with an unusual look on her face. If you have a defectiveness, abandonment, or mistrust schema, you may jump to conclusions or predict loss and rejection whenever you feel someone is unhappy with you. So, you're likely to assume your supervisor is upset with you and instantly experience a knot in your stomach, a pounding heart, and a voice in your head that says, *That's it; I'm fired.* Even if you have a keen facility for reasonable thinking and testing reality and can produce no evidence to make the case that you're being fired, you'll still feel queasiness and dread because beneath the rational surface lies the schema. Like an infection, the schema doesn't respond to the first round of practical interventions. You may ultimately—and frequently—find your negative expectations unwarranted but still be unable to halt the careening process once a schema is triggered. You may even recognize it as a vaguely familiar unease, reminiscent of something but unsure of its origins.

Our brains are primed to launch protective missiles when an enemy is present, and in this case the schema is the enemy. Ironically, while seeking refuge from this predator, we often end up right back in its grip.

Again, let's consider that "funny look" on your supervisor's face: If your particular potion for eradicating this sense of doom is to flee to safety, you might avoid tasks, become preoccupied and distracted, make mistakes, share the gloom with colleagues, and ultimately actually put your job at risk. You could receive disciplinary action for a decline in performance, having shifted into an avoidant and distracted coping mode. If you have an abandonment schema—always expecting loss and rejection—you may, despite your attempts to dodge it, end up chanting the old familiar verses of the schema. (Recall the woman with the abandonment schema whose [not narcissistic] husband had to travel for business. Her fears led to unreasonable demands for contact and reassurance, which could ultimately damage the relationship and result in yet another loss. Not her fault; just a replay of painful past events she cannot distinguish from the here and now.)

In extreme cases, if your fears and self-protective measures become chronic patterns in the workplace, you might actually get fired. Self-fulfilling prophecy? No. Ironic? No. Guided by impulse, you are a creature of habit, unknowingly navigating toward the familiar, even those very painful familiar feelings you seek to avoid. You need to stop dodging the bullets unless you determine that they are indeed bullets. But stopping your habitual behavior will feel counterintuitive.

We are all primed for survival, but it isn't always clear what represents a genuine threat. Dealing with a narcissist can abduct your sense of discernment, leaving you feeling like you're forever facing a charging grizzly bear or the barren aloneness of a dark cave. The goal is to distinguish genuine threats from schemas that distort your perceptions and responses. To do this, you need to make the implicit more explicit; you need to become aware of inner motivations in a way that is deeply felt, not just intellectually understood. Chapter 5 offers detailed exercises using mindfulness strategies to help you differentiate threat from challenge and harness a felt sense of your motivational engines, which drive your response patterns.

Louis's Story

Louis, a fifty-eight-year-old man, provides a good example of the self-perpetuating dilemmas a narcissist faces. One of Louis's schemas is defectiveness/shame. In childhood, Louis developed a deeply held (though not explicitly conscious) feeling that he was inadequate and unlovable. He and his wife, Francine, have been married for thirty-two years. They have two grown sons, both married and living in other cities. About two years ago, Louis retired from a Fortune 100 company. A highly successful man, he is widely recognized and respected in his field, and he's attained impressive financial security. Francine is a schoolteacher who continues to enjoy her work and has no desire to retire anytime soon.

Francine came to see me hoping I would work with Louis and perhaps with the two of them together. Francine had become fairly sturdy in her compassionate understanding of Louis, thanks to her own therapy and self-help efforts. She had also deepened her self-awareness and developed skills for asserting herself. Feeling more equipped, she'd been able to confront Louis on more than thirty years of critical, self-absorbed, avoidant, and obnoxious behaviors. She also identified her own struggle with compliance and passivity in her relationship with Louis, as well as with others.

Unfortunately, despite her candor and devotion, nothing was changing. She prepared herself for the possibility of separation if Louis wouldn't consent to therapy and finally gave him an ultimatum. Louis was no stranger to therapy. He had "visited" therapists many times. It was always short-lived. Francine would minimize her complaints or Louis would mow down the therapist with his unyielding sarcasm and intimidation. But Francine made it clear to Louis that if things didn't change this time, she would leave him. Having heard that I was an expert in high-conflict relationships and narcissism, Francine saw this as their one last chance—no pressure, of course—to save their marriage.

Louis is an attractive, well-dressed, and well-educated man who sports expensive loafers and proudly mentions his abundant library of classic literature. He enjoys name-dropping. When not playing tennis or golf, Louis is mostly engaged in solitary activities like reading, surfing the Web, or managing his investment portfolio. His few friends are mostly through Francine. Even his tennis and golf mates are former business acquaintances to whom he has little personal attachment. His sons call him, but mainly for business advice and for loans. He misses them.

Louis would like Francine to retire so they could travel more. He is adamantly disinterested in her enthusiasm for her work. He is insulting and puts her down, admonishing her "simple" profession. But now Louis is worried and agitated because Francine has threatened to leave him and she seems serious. For the first time, the stakes are really high and there is leverage for change.

Leverage and Incentive

Leverage comes in many forms: a potential or actual significant loss (such as a loved one's threat to leave), a disabling medical condition, retirement, termination of a job, financial instability, legal challenges, or sometimes even the ache of loneliness, depression, or the isolation that comes with the passage of time. With leverage, the possibility for insight and change emerges. Incentive also helps, though it isn't as easy to cultivate. To the narcissist, achieving shame-free and secure connections, a sense of belonging, and liberation from having to constantly prove his self-worth probably sounds good. But without experience to draw upon and plenty of success with excessive autonomy, these incentives are likely to seem unattainable and even unimaginable. I often tell my narcissistic clients who aren't changing that it's either because they aren't in enough pain yet or don't have anything tangible to reach for except an unrelenting desire for fame and glory. They also have a firm "wall" of emotional detachment that prohibits any connection with their vulnerability. This was true for Louis throughout his marriage, but now, for the first time in his adult life, he was experiencing enough pain and fear that the wall might actually come down and change was possible.

Louis's Schemas in Action

Louis's schemas are easily triggered in social settings, such as on the golf course with Jack, a former business colleague. Trying not to feel shame and rejection, Louis postures himself in approval-seeking mode, aggrandizing himself with incessant talk about his standing at the club. At first, Jack may be amused or impressed by the content and gallant style of Louis's speech. But inevitably he grows tired, and annoyed, and ends up thinking, *Who does he think he is? What a self-centered bore. Somebody get me out of here!* Louis, in the mighty grip of his defectiveness/shame schema, has inspired the very thing he was trying to avoid: rejection and disapproval. The stirrings of the schema and the automatic decision to hide it through show-off behaviors simply perpetuate it.

So, you might ask, is Louis simply a masochist, or are all humans hopelessly at the mercy of habitual beliefs? Neither. To grasp the power and possibility of change, we need to look at the intricate and elegant apparatus of the brain and how it relates to both nature (genetic precursors like temperament) and nurture (the security or lack thereof within the parent-child relationship and the overall environment of the developing child).

Foundations of Security: Biology and Attachment

Daniel J. Siegel, a child psychiatrist, an expert in family dynamics, and a leader in the development of interpersonal neurobiology, proposes that childhood attachment experiences directly influence emotions, behavior, autobiographical memory, and one's personal narrative. He's written several influential books addressing these topics, including *The Developing Mind* (2001), *Parenting from the Inside Out* (Siegel and Hartzell 2004), and

The Mindful Brain (2007), and many more. Although Siegel's focus isn't narcissists, his theories shed a great deal of light on this personality type.

Attachment and the Brain

Siegel's work is informed by a thoughtful examination of theories of attachment, neurobiology, parent-child relationships, and mindful awareness. His discoveries in interpersonal neurobiology offer an innovative guidepost for those trying to make sense out of their reactions to the world and who are seeking evidence for the possibility of personal growth and change. Siegel offers an enlightening and accessible tutorial on the intricate assemblage of our most profound personal labyrinth: the brain. Like Jeffrey Young, he points the needle of the compass toward a combination of parent-child relationship and the native capacities of the child.

Siegel also helps us appreciate how our extraordinary brains connect us with memory-driven states of mind in seconds. For example, you might drift back to a loving and nostalgic memory of your grandma and her delicious apple pies as you encounter a similar wondrous aroma wafting out of a bakery. The mind also has the power to retrieve the sadness linked with a tucked-away memory of rejection. For example, while trying to capture your spouse's attention as he scans his phone at a restaurant, you may unconsciously recall your father, who was too busy to notice your longing to be hugged, and find yourself gripped by a sudden melancholic twinge.

You know the feeling: You're driving and a song comes on the radio that suddenly transports you to another time and place, maybe a first love or a first loss. Your body fills with sensations and heightened awareness. You don't always immediately know why you are feeling that way. It may take a while to pluck the memory from your archives. But your brain is way ahead of your mind, making connections to what might sound, taste, smell, look, or feel like something you've experienced before. It is the grand master of association and meaning, but it doesn't assess everything correctly. It's like the old game Concentration, where you lay picture cards facedown and then turn them over two at a time, trying to find a matched pair. Your brain is primed to probe its memory files in search of that which has been experienced, observed, and stored. It is the library of your personal experience.

When you access memory, you access your imagination, intuition, learning, and logical thinking. Your internal environment is both stable and ever changing. Memory makes you able to adapt, learn new things, and attach meaning to experiences. In its quest for familiarity and stability, your brain constantly asks, *What does that mean?*—though this often occurs without your awareness. It is memory that offers the navigational assistance as you drive a familiar route, allowing you to listen to the radio, sip your coffee, and hardly pay attention. You know the way; it is automatically summoned from your reference file.

However, should you encounter a detour sign, you will put down your coffee, turn down the radio, and sharpen your focus. This is an example of your brain seeking the familiar and predictable. Suddenly, with your attention fully engaged and deliberately focused on the moment, you look for those orange signs that point you toward a recognizable landmark, putting you back on track. You breathe easier when you figure it out. We are all pleasure seekers relying on the power of the brain (which is primed to avoid pain) to help us find our way out of uncomfortable situations.

So, what does this have to do with narcissism? Your experiences, along with your innate drive, tendencies, and idiosyncratic makeup, are filed in many categorical memory folders in your brain. Among the folders one is titled "How I get to work each day." Another is "How I feel and what I do when I'm with an obnoxious person who needs constant admiration, makes me feel small or invisible, and has to be right about everything." And, when you encounter Mr. Charming in the office on Monday, your expectations and reactions are predetermined by the content of that memory folder. You might, however, actively engage your brain in seeking out a different route.

In AA meetings, there is a saying that goes something like this: The definition of insanity is doing the exact same thing over and over again and expecting a different result. No, you're not insane. But it sometimes feels that way when nothing changes despite your tenacious efforts. Harnessing a keen awareness of your present moment and trying a new approach can feel awkward and unnatural, given your past experiences. If you're a people pleaser who never rocks the boat, it can be difficult to imagine taking a different approach. The history of your experience is powerful and can dominate your reactions, but it isn't necessarily relevant to the here and now. Just because someone once intimidated you into maintaining peace at all costs or believing you have nothing important to say doesn't mean it's true now. It wasn't true then either, but as a child, your ability to forge your own beliefs and choose your responses was limited. You did the best you could as a child, but you can make new choices as an adult—not so easy when faced with the off-putting reactions of narcissists, but doable and necessary.

Creatures of Habit

As humans, we are essentially guided by memories, both explicit (the ones we vividly recall) and implicit (the ones we remember without knowing we're remembering them). This concept validates the ideas that Jeffrey Young proposes in schema theory and allows us to probe where life themes reside within the brain—in explicit or implicit memory. Our schemas, or personal life themes, often wind up in the implicit storage container, outside of our awareness. When they're triggered, we may become aware of bodily, emotional, and cognitive shifts without a clear perception of the underlying memories, and perhaps without even understanding that memories are responsible. This causes us to feel childlike and powerless, igniting the well-designed mechanics of moving from threat to safety.

Living in a triggered state is like living in a "once upon a time" place where sensory reenactments of an early experience eclipse the present moment. When feeling at risk or sensing a threat, we usually turn to familiar strategies to banish our demons, soothe the soul, and recast our appearance to the world. Within the wardrobe of your brain, you have many vintage costumes to outfit your states of mind and camouflage your discomfort; some of us become vengeful warriors, some become do-gooders or self-righteous preachers, and yet others become perilous perfectionists or unstoppable intellectualizers. At times, we also show up as healthy grown-up folks with rational reactions grounded in the here and now.

Young Louis: The Burgeoning Narcissist

Louis, discussed earlier in this chapter, grew up with a critical and demanding father and a socially preoccupied mother. The oldest of four children, he became a companion to his mom during his dad's extended business travels and long workdays. Louis was smart, a very good athlete, and was highly praised for his achievements. Because he was the oldest and his mother was so distracted, Louis had few limits placed upon him. He was raised to believe that he was special and that any problems were "the other guy's fault."

His dad made it known that no son of his would dare embarrass him with less-than-perfect grades or a less-than-perfect performance in any public setting. His dad also made it quite clear that any expression of fear or sadness was a sign of weakness. So, Louis courageously endured countless nights of sitting alone at home, studying or practicing his clarinet—which he hated—while his parents took the younger children out for ice cream or other special treats. Louis was constantly told that he was bound for great things; he was special. Loneliness was familiar to him, whether he was alone or among others. He had poor interpersonal skills because his primary role models were myopically focused on achievement and self-control. Within his family, he had no examples of empathy or emotional connectedness to others.

As an adolescent, Louis was awkward with girls. He masked his shame with academic competitiveness and solitary activities, including grandiose fantasies of fame and fortune. Before long, Louis's maladaptive schemas, which included emotional deprivation, defectiveness/shame, mistrust, entitlement, and approval seeking, became the wallpaper of his internal life.

Connecting the Dots

Louis, like many others with these issues, was determined to create a life that would afford him enough self-sufficiency to shelter him from the longings and loneliness of his past. But the brain is an unyielding concierge that insists on unrequested wake-up calls, free from the responsibility of attending to the undernourished soul. Human beings are wired for love and connection to others, and the brain will strive to achieve these goals despite the roadblocks that schemas present.

Researchers in the field of parent-child attachment provide much data to support this truth. And so it is with Louis, who repeatedly hits snooze on his internal wake-up call and instead moves aggressively through life disguised in his impeccably starched veneer. He racks up his extraordinary references, displays magnanimous goals, and indulges in solitary soothing—all in the service of not feeling the "shameful little weakling" held hostage beneath his skin. His impatience with "lesser mortals" and "small talk" leaves him barely able to notice the impact of his boorish behavior on others who might love him and long to be loved by him. Louis moves in a world of extraordinariness where any experience of being ordinary or being surrounded by ordinary people, places, and events is the equivalent of being emotionally helpless, needy, defective, and unworthy. The demand to don the cloak of uniqueness and superiority, once externally driven by the needs and demands of his parents, has become entirely internalized and self-imposed.

We examine these origins in the spirit of holding narcissists accountable, not for feeling sorry for them. This understanding allows for lowering the self-aggrandized pedestal they've placed themselves upon and peering into the deeper regions of their soul. As a therapist, my compassion is reserved for connecting to the vulnerable child, the one who suffers beneath the bluster.

Conclusion

In combination with biological makeup, early experience can dramatically shape our impressions, beliefs, and responses vis-à-vis the world we live in. We are creatures of habit who gravitate toward the familiar, and our early maladaptive schemas can be like a boomerang leading us back to where we started. Understanding the finely honed mechanisms of the brain gives us an appreciation for how cumbersome change is, while also affirming that change is possible. For all of us, grasping and accepting the anatomical realities of memory and its associational tendencies can help mediate obstacles to change, like shame and self-blame.

If the narcissist in your life is amenable to seeking professional help, look for a therapist who can be empathically attuned and sturdily confrontational. In a limited but necessary way, the therapist must reparent the wounded side of the narcissist. If you choose to seek professional assistance for yourself, the therapist should be able to escort you through an excavation of your own schemas and idiosyncratic obstacles to healthy assertiveness. Your therapist must help bolster you against reluctance or resignation so that you can make healthy and wise choices for yourself when dealing with the narcissist. In my experience, this approach loosens the clutch of a long-standing sense of shame and hopelessness—not just for you, but also for the narcissist. Your authentic self can emerge, grounded in wisdom, empathy, and self-advocacy, and the narcissist, under some conditions, can become connected, receptive, and responsible. This approach enhances the possibility for healing the hurt and engaging the lonely and precious exiled parts of both of you.

CHAPTER 3

Getting Captured:
Identifying Your Personal Traps

And since you know you cannot see yourself,
so well as by reflection, I, your glass,
will modestly discover to yourself,
that of yourself which you yet know not of.

—William Shakespeare

Now that you've sharpened your understanding of the origins of narcissism, its manifestations, and its related schemas, let's point the lens toward you. When under the narcissist's spell, you may not see clearly what is happening in your mind and body. You may feel ineffective and unsatisfied with your ways of dealing with this trying person. You're not alone. In my practice, clients in similar situations repeatedly ask:

- What's wrong with me? Am I simply a masochist?

- How can I allow myself to be played the fool?

- Why am I so drawn to these difficult people?

- Am I being punished?

- How do these types of people always find me?

- Do I have "doormat" written on my forehead?

- Why can't I just speak up and tell him to...?

It can be difficult to assess toxic interactions during early phases of any relationship, particularly if you're only together from time to time. Even when he is a bit obnoxious, you may have grown up with the message *Buck up and just deal with it* implanted in your brain, especially if the narcissist in your life happens to be an authority figure, such as a boss, supervisor, professor, or even a romantic partner. You aren't foolish or being punished, and you definitely don't have a self-defeating label emblazoned on your brow. The narcissist's charm and wit can be very hypnotizing, encouraging forgiveness even when he's out of line. You're drawn to this person because he is attractive in some ways. No one is immune to the spell that the narcissist so deftly casts. It can be difficult to speak up. The costs may appear too great, and if you've been in the relationship for a while, you've been well trained in the art of diplomacy—or, rather, biting your tongue.

Comfort Zones: The Challenges of Living with and Changing Your Habits

Despite the well-worn soles, poor support, and unsightly appearance of our comfortable old shoes, we choose to keep them because they have come to fit us well, customized by the memory of our foot's every movement. We feel we can endure long walks in these shoes because of their familiar fit. This is also the case with our relationships and our styles of relating with others. When faced with a difficult situation, we're likely to rely on what we know—the automatic patterns programmed into our brain's response system. It's only when the "heel comes loose" in a relationship, or the pain becomes too great, that we begin to experience depression, anxiety, and stress. Once things become this painful, despite the discomfort, we may be willing to break out of our comfort zone and either repair those old shoes or toss them out.

Your early experience of the world—from navigating the continent of your crib to scaling the slope of your mother's lap to negotiating the playground—provided many thoughts and sensations that you have collected and stored in your memory library. Retrieval of these souvenirs, such as what might happen when you cry, laugh, or show fear or anger, and what to do about it, requires little effort given the repetitious nature of so much of our experience and how predictable the outcomes often are. From our early years as helpless little beings, our travels are fraught with countless letdowns and emotional compromises, but, in the process, we become equipped with a compass for survival.

We learn quickly what we can expect from the world, from the people in it, and from ourselves. The well-designed architectural landscape of the brain is expansive, providing countless rooms for thoughts, feelings, behaviors, and bodily sensations. Experience is the concierge of the mind, discreetly guiding us from room to room.

Why the Narcissist Triggers You

Take a few moments to look back at the eighteen schemas described in chapter 2 and once again identify your schemas. You will likely find that several of the schemas seem to fit. It's very common for schemas to occur in clusters. Some of the groupings most common among people in relationships with narcissists are mistrust and subjugation; defectiveness and unrelenting standards; and abandonment, emotional deprivation, and self-sacrifice. Let's take a closer look at those three clusters.

Mistrust and Subjugation

You might identify with the mistrust and subjugation schemas if your emotional narrative tells the story of a child who was taken advantage of or mistreated. As such, your reaction to manipulative or abusive people is to subjugate yourself by tucking in your feelings and doing what you're told. If you had no one to protect you as a child, this may have been the only reasonable way to survive. Now that you're an adult, when the narcissist in your life becomes controlling or demanding or puts you down with criticism and blame, your old memories are fired up (beneath your actual awareness), along with habitual reactions.

Your protective mechanisms cause you to respond to the control and abuse by shutting down and doing what you're told. The problem with this system is that the long-choreographed movements of childhood are now in need of an adult makeover. Anchored in the past, habitual beliefs and responses become outdated and self-defeating, yet they can hold you hostage. As a result, you may lose your voice and forfeit your rights.

Defectiveness and Unrelenting Standards

If you have defectiveness and unrelenting standards schemas, you may have felt unlovable, inadequate, or flawed as a child. In response, you likely worked hard to be good and acceptable and to get it right to avoid criticism, achieve acceptance, and enjoy the loving attention that every child longs for.

Now, when the narcissist in your life is critical or withholding, you work tirelessly to be the perfect friend, spouse, coworker, or sibling. Unfortunately, and without realizing it, you begin dancing to that distant drummer within an orchestra of familiar melodies.

Abandonment, Emotional Deprivation, and Self-Sacrifice

You may have abandonment, emotional deprivation, and self-sacrifice schemas if you grew up feeling that there was no one you could truly count on, the people you loved could leave you, or they would never truly understand or love you. You may have arrived at these beliefs due to the instability of an alcoholic parent, the loss of a caregiver, a divorce, or perhaps a parent who was too self-absorbed, passive, or even depressed to nurture you adequately.

Through a combination of temperament and experience, you may have put your needs aside to focus on taking care of others. If you felt like a burden to your parents and were sensitive to their upsets and expectations, you probably worked hard to please them (and others), asking for little in return and enjoying whatever crumbs came your way. Any resentment about being deprived or abandoned was eclipsed by an ever-presiding sense of guilt and loyalty. Craig Malkin, bestselling author of the book *Rethinking Narcissism*, brilliantly captures the essence of this in his popularized use of the term "echoism".

As a result, when dealing with the narcissist in your life, you carefully walk the narrow, eggshell-lined path, keeping your own needs tucked away. Fearful of losing him or igniting his short fuse, you give in, unintentionally enabling him, and sacrificing your own needs. Until, of course, your wise and hungry mind tunes in, filling you with resentment and launching you into a "what about me" outburst. Unfortunately, this anger may set you up for a fiery reaction from the narcissist, "how dare you" voice your hurts and longings, and—ta-da!—you return to your familiar post of guilt and surrender.

Developing an Authentic Voice

Of course, it may be that when you find yourself tested or triggered by difficult interactions with *you-know-who*, you find it hard to resist fighting back with bullying, demanding, or threatening tones. And while you have the right to express your frustration and be heard, the primary opponent in your battle is sometimes a phantom: the enemy emerging from your memory's archives. Your buttons get pushed, and you counterattack or get defensive. The narcissist can tempt you into battle with guns blazing against a backdrop of childhood suffering. There is a difference between taking a stand for yourself—utilizing an authentic and assertive voice against abuse, control, and oppression—and defending yourself with contempt, criticalness, and self-righteousness, the dance of the narcissist. You have a right to be heard, and that can only happen when you change the dance.

Let's go back to Louis from chapter 2. As he launches one of his usual degrading assaults on his wife, Francine, she feels her emotional deprivation and self-sacrifice schemas getting fired up. However, she feels this in the form of tenseness in her jaw, queasiness in her gut, and heat rising into her face. She hears her inner voice saying, *I am sick of forever doing and giving but getting nothing back. I've never gotten my needs met, and I never will. I've had it!* And now Francine, sturdy with her righteous anger, attempts to fight back declaring, "I've been a good wife. I've done my best, but you never appreciate anything. You're inhuman; you're the loser." She slams the door and heads for the bedroom, where she will cry alone yet again. At first glance, we may cheer for her as she courageously takes on her inimitable partner: "You go, girl!"

However, Louis's stunned reaction becomes a shrug and a smirk. If you could listen to his thinking, you would hear something like this: *There she goes again. Must be that time of the month…hormonal imbalance.*

Oh well, she'll get over it. She'll see that I'm right. She has such limited insight. It's hard for her to handle the truth. Yikes!

So close, but... What Louis didn't get (and it's not easy for narcissists to get, even when it is eloquently delivered) was that Francine feels lonely and misunderstood in this relationship, and that his angry tone and demeaning treatment are unacceptable and she won't tolerate them anymore. He probably isn't even aware that Francine understands his inability to express his needs without feeling weak or ashamed. He didn't hear that she would love to share more time and intimacy with him, but that it's impossible for her to wrap her arms around the fire-breathing dragon he's become. He didn't hear that she feels hurt, even though she knows he probably doesn't mean to hurt her, and that she needs him to be more responsible for the impact of his words and tone. He doesn't understand that although she knows he loves her, that simply isn't good enough anymore. And he never heard about her own struggle with a dysfunctional life pattern or that she isn't going to dance this dance with him anymore. He must be held accountable for his actions, which is hard to do when you're caught up in anger.

Louis demands special attention from Francine and has unreasonable expectations. Nina Brown, an expert on narcissism, writes, "Everyone can appreciate feeling unique and special from time to time. Indeed, one of the reasons we fall in love or become attracted to someone is their ability to make us feel that way. However, the person who has an excessive need to feel unique and special expects *everyone* to make them feel that way all of the time. They can be easily displeased or even angered when others do not act to make them feel unique and special" (2001, 27).

Unfortunately, Francine wasn't directly engaged in a confrontation with Louis's unreasonable demands and unremitting criticisms. She was triggered, distracted, and engaged in a phantom war with her parents. She had shifted into the frightened little girl mode, whose mother left and whose father worked all the time, who had to sacrifice her needs and desires to care for her younger sister. That little girl, now turned feisty and defiant, was doing battle with the long-held belief that she must suck it up. No matter how justified her feelings, the way she expressed herself didn't serve her in the present. Instead, she was captured by an old pattern. As she works to summon new strength, she will need to get those unmet needs met, those schemas healed, so she can engage in the battle to be waged in the here and now, with Louis, who often exasperates her and who would test anyone's interpersonal capacities and emotional energy. Remember, almost no one can push people's buttons like the narcissist can.

This is not to say that the failed communication was Francine's fault. She did the best she could in one of her most challenging and important relationships. She worked hard to believe that she matters and struggled to obtain emotional reciprocity from Louis. The ratio of give to get in their relationship has always been off, and she's begun to recognize her role in this, having unknowingly agreed to surrender and sacrifice her own needs in the hope that he would someday appreciate her and love her better.

Francine has felt trapped for years, being a teacher with a minimal income and the mother of two children. She was committed to raising her sons in an intact family, sparing them from a broken home like she had. Her liabilities and fears were her anchors; she wouldn't run as her mother had. For a long time, she had felt herself to be a virtuous victim for putting up with Louis. Now she's struggling to be compassionate with herself, given her limited options, her fear, and her genuine (but dimming) love for this man who has been so disappointing to her in so many ways.

Francine, like many spouses of narcissists, believes in the humanness and woundedness of her partner. She's witnessed his stumbling efforts to tell her he loves her and look after her when she's faced difficulties. She knows his story and feels a deep love for the vulnerable part of him who lives in exile. But it isn't her responsibility, nor is it within her power, to change Louis. To impact the path he chooses, she may only light the torch and lead the way, change the dance, or drop some new seeds in the soil by speaking of that which is unacceptable and the potential for grave consequences for their relationship. But she doesn't intend to carry the burden indefinitely without seeing improvements in Louis's emotional intimacy, reciprocity, respect, and empathy.

A Game of Collusion

Psychotherapist Sandy Hotchkiss, an expert in personality disorders, writes, "For narcissists, competition of all kinds is a way to reaffirm superiority, although many will only compete when they anticipate a favorable outcome" (2003, 13). Louis, knowing Francine tends to choke up during a plea for tenderness, could easily mow her down with a lofty speech on gender differences and displaced female angst. He always wins the game of never getting her point and never feeling her pain. He's always been able to count on her business-as-usual behavior once things cooled down. In fact, he is a master at this game with most people. His assistant, Beth, who worked for him for ten years, tells the story of how Louis could make you doubt the very color of the blouse you were wearing. His personal trainer, Bill, tells of times when Louis would keep him waiting for nearly twenty minutes, then inevitably convince him that it was the rigid policy of the gym that was faulty, not Louis's time management.

What do all three of these people—Francine, Beth, and Bill—have in common that allows Louis to be such an unstoppable gaslighter and disarming champ in their interactions? In his presence, all three of them frequently experience intimidation, resignation, and self-doubt. Though Louis's personality is a big factor, Francine, Beth, and Bill all have their own schemas that play a role in the painful dynamic of their relationships with Louis. Let's take a closer look to illuminate this common thread. As you read their stories, try to identify any elements that feel relevant to your experience with the narcissist in your life.

Bill, the Trainer

Bill frequently falls victim to the "Louis-es" of the world, but his own traps of failure, subjugation, and defectiveness are actually his greatest opponents. He is triggered by Louis's colossal vocabulary, his deep and sonorous voice, and the impressive financial accomplishments Louis boasts of during his workouts. Because he fears feeling rejected or less intelligent, Bill pushes his own opinions to the far corners of his mind.

Louis triggers in Bill the memory of being teased and bullied for not being able to keep up with the more aggressive kids at school. Pressured to put up or shut up when it came to competition, he chose to shut up—probably a good decision back then, given that Bill had no real advocate to guide or protect him. Bill's dad was a workaholic who was never around, and his mom was very ill during much of his childhood. His grandma told him that he was a good boy but a bit too weak, just like his grandpa, who died when Bill was a baby. All of these discordant melodies from his childhood continue to resonate in his thirty-two-year-old brain, and the automatic reflex to dodge enemies from his past reemerges. Bill forgets that he's an amazing personal trainer, well respected by his peers and clients alike. While he would like to maintain Louis as his client, he doesn't need to tolerate his disrespect and self-righteous domination.

Beth, the Administrative Assistant

Beth, a forty-four-year-old woman who has risen in the ranks of the company that brought so much fame and fortune to Louis, is a bright and hardworking person who generously gives of her time and creative energy both at work and at home. Despite her prestigious education and achievements, Beth's ego is all too easily erased in the face of powerful authority figures. Louis was one such figure. Her father was another.

Beth grew up in a small town. She was the youngest of five children and the pièce de résistance in her father's eyes. In fact, hiding from her father's ever-present gaze was a challenge for young Beth. Her dad demanded a great deal of attention from her and denied her the ordinary privileges of a young girl. He was unrelenting in his expectations that she should be the best at everything. As an adolescent, Beth was a bit of a jouster, and when she disagreed with her father, pleading for a normal life, her temerity in challenging her father's "wisdom" and authority was met by his smoldering stare, heartbroken displeasure, and irrefutably punitive voice. Because she enjoyed her father's fondness and feared the guilt she felt when she upset him, Beth eventually resigned herself to gazing up at the pedestal she placed him on, trading her personal needs for maintaining peace in his heart, much like her mom had done.

Beth earned many academic honors and recognition, including high school valedictorian and merit scholarships for college. She often recalled the proud look on her father's face—an immigrant whose dream was to see his children go to college and have a better life than his own—when she strode by him in her cap and gown on graduation day. In a brief interview, she told me, "His happiness in that moment felt like it was worth all the loneliness, not choosing my own clothes, and all the missed parties, dates, and movies."

So, what's wrong with that story, you might ask? The lack of balance and an authentically defined self. Beth's emotional legacy was an inability to have a genuine sense of herself and a tendency to feel she had to be what others needed her to be, which left her constantly running from the guilt associated with letting people down or disappointing them. She even feared that she might bequeath these traits to her daughters. Even now, when she runs into Louis, Beth can feel tightness in her stomach and nervousness in her throat as she prepares her curtsy for the mighty master, ready to agree with whatever he might utter.

Wendy, the Therapist

Okay, now it's my turn. Early in therapy, Louis had a habit of being five to ten minutes late and then demanding more time at the end of the session. "What's the big deal about giving me five to ten more minutes? This is important! You're just like every other therapist, or even lawyers for that matter. It's a business: time's up, pay up. I feel I should have a few extra minutes when I need it." Sometimes he would just ignore me and continue to talk right past my announcement that the session was over. Given that many therapists tend to have self-sacrifice or subjugation schemas, or both, the task of being assertive and setting limits can be an onerous one.

I had to find a way to push past my anger and resentment at Louis's sense of entitlement, as well as my tendency to feel guilty when not giving in to his demands. Finally, I harnessed my awareness of little Louis's need to feel special to feel cared for, and his experience of getting his way for years, and told him, "Louis, if what you mean is that I couldn't possibly care about you given the time limitations of our session, consider this: You can only pay me for my time and expertise; the caring is free. Even you cannot make me care about you. And I must tell you that when you speak to me as you just did, it's hard for me to feel my caring for you. I wonder if this is what it's like for Francine and your sons."

I tried to communicate that I didn't view the situation as his fault, but that his behavior is his responsibility. I said, "I know it's hard for you, given that you grew up without adequate experiences of tolerating feelings of disappointment or frustration, and because you were led to believe that you were superior to other people and entitled to special privileges. You were taught that the rules for everyone else don't really apply to you. So, it isn't your fault, Louis. But to have the kinds of relationships you want, you must work on these beliefs and behaviors or you'll keep driving people away from you. Let's try it again: Tell me about the disappointment you feel when our time is up. What is it you want me to know?"

Louis managed to listen with a minimum of eye-rolling, sighed, and, with difficulty, replied, "The time seems to go by very quickly, and sometimes—okay, often—I want to be here longer, to finish a thought or to tell you about something else, and it's frustrating to have to stop when you say so. I end up feeling like I'm being rejected or controlled, even though I do believe that you're trying to help me." I thanked him for his courageous openness and assured him that I understood why he felt that way, given his life themes and the inherent limitations of a therapy relationship.

I asked him, "How uncomfortable was it for you to say it that way, Louis?" He replied, "It's just unnatural, and I have to think about it. It's tedious and a little annoying." Even Louis smirked at having said this, recognizing the arrogance of the statement. I suggested that it's an unfamiliar way of being in the world, one that requires paying closer attention to the feelings of listeners, as well as his own unacknowledged and important feelings—something he wasn't used to. Louis agreed with this assessment. I let him know that it was hard for me to ask him to leave, but it wouldn't be fair to my other clients if I didn't. Then I reminded him that it was hard for me to care for him when I felt like he was ignoring my rights and criticizing my intentions unfairly. Louis nodded. He got it. We then collaborated on a plan to be mindful of time limitations and his vulnerability. In addition, Louis agreed to make a better effort to arrive on time for his sessions.

In schema therapy, leverage is important for working successfully with narcissists. Jeffrey Young describes it like this: "The therapist strives to keep patients in touch with their emotional suffering because as soon as the suffering is gone, they are likely to leave treatment. The more the therapist keeps patients aware of their inner emptiness, feelings of defectiveness, and loneliness, the more the therapist has leverage for keeping them in treatment.... The therapist also focuses on the negative consequences of the patient's narcissism, such as rejection by loved ones or setbacks in one's career.... The emotional connection to the therapist and fear of reprisal from others are the main motivators for continuing in therapy" (Young, Klosko, and Weishaar 2006, 395).

exercise: The Burden, Not the Blame

Are you ready to take on the burden of change without the blame—to accept that even if your schemas aren't your fault, you are responsible for your behavior now, as an adult? Though it may seem a bit scary or overwhelming, this opens the door to transformation. This exercise will help you examine your own schemas and coping modes and identify healthy and assertive ways of responding to replace old patterns of behavior. This will be good for you, and there's a good chance that your clear communication will help as you begin to disarm the narcissist. In this exercise, you'll also consider any leverage you might have for getting the attention of the narcissist in your life and positioning that person for change. Here's an example:

> **Your schemas:** *Abandonment, defectiveness, self-sacrifice, and subjugation.*
>
> **Effects of your schemas:** *I take the blame, feel inadequate, and believe that it's better to put my needs on the back burner and be silent than to speak out, get it wrong, and possibly end up all alone.*
>
> **Your coping modes:** *Giving in and avoiding.*
>
> **The truth:** *It isn't my fault. We both play a role in the conflict. I am capable of being responsible, and besides, I'm already so alone because I don't have a sense of self, a voice, or a meaningful connection with my husband.*
>
> **Healthy assertive message:** *I will not be treated this way. It's unacceptable, even if it isn't your intention to hurt me.*
>
> **Leverage:** *I know that my husband doesn't want to lose me. I'm willing to start communicating about the option of leaving—not as a threat, but as a necessary choice if things don't change between us.*

Using the structure set forth in that example, take a fresh piece of paper and write about your own schemas and coping modes, then consider the truth of the situation. Take some time to develop a healthy assertive message—one that neither cowers before nor attacks the narcissist in your life. Finally, take some time to consider what leverage you might bring to bear to enlist the narcissist in making changes to improve your relationship.

Hope Springs Eternal: The Capacity to Learn and Change

Without a magic wand, the options for resolving conflicts in relationships are finite: ending the relationship, sticking with the status quo, adopting new dysfunctional patterns, or working it out in a healthy way. The last of these is obviously best if you wish to stay in the relationship, but it requires an exhausting commitment, even when both parties are fully enlisted in the process of change. But rest assured: all is not lost. While the challenge may seem daunting, the possibilities for repair exist.

The brain is capable of change, and therefore our personalities are flexible and open to change as well. Experts propose that one pathway to change may come from attuned listening and genuine self-expression within the context of a conscious, here-and-now state of mind. Dan Siegel uses the term "contingent communication" to describe this approach: "In contingent communication the receiver of the message listens with an open mind and with all his or her senses. Her reaction is dependent on what was actually communicated, not on a predetermined and rigid mental model of what was expected" (Siegel and Hartzell 2004, 81).

Siegel goes on to illustrate the essence of "feeling felt" in terms of the parent-child relationship: "When we send out a signal, our brains are receptive to the responses of others to that signal. The responses we receive become embedded in the neural maps of our core sense of self.... The responses of others are not merely mirroring our own signals but incorporate the essence of the other person's view, which makes sense of our communication. In this manner, children come to feel felt: they come to feel as if their mind exists in the mind of their parent" (Siegel and Hartzell 2004, 83). What a soothing connection—to feel truly "gotten," to sense that you are held accurately and safely in the mind of another. Think about it: Who truly gets you?

A healthy relationship is a reciprocal one whereby both members feel accurately seen and carried in the mind of the other. Where both parties feel safe and trusted. Where no one has to prove their worth. Where both parties graciously attend to the bids for love and understanding.

Conclusion

Within the context of "felt" connections, we are afforded the chance to achieve mental and emotional shifts that lead to new interpretations and actions regarding self-worth and our relationships with others. These connections offer us the possibility of forming new habits and freeing ourselves from automatic reflexes linked to the past. So, the task is to establish this sort of connection with the narcissist in your life, whether that person is a boss, coworker, family member, neighbor, friend, spouse, or lover.

Unfortunately, these last two are usually the most resistant to change, given the enormity of importance of the relationship and how heartily entrenched schemas can be. But by establishing a more "felt" connection, you open the door to repairing your sense of self, and to the possibility of utilizing your repertoire of skills to influence, improve, and even transform your relationship with the narcissist. And, if that isn't possible, you hone the skills for setting necessary limits in the relationship or ending it. The following chapters will help you sharpen your awareness, harness your courage, and maintain your emotional energy while developing the skills you need for creating effective outcomes when dealing with the narcissist in your life.

CHAPTER 4

Overcoming the Obstacles: *Communication Pitfalls, Snags, and Glitches*

It is one of the most beautiful compensations of life that no man can sincerely try to help another without helping himself.

—Ralph Waldo Emerson

Now you can define narcissism, how it affects the life of the narcissist, and how that acerbic behavior impacts those who must deal with him or her (something you were probably all too familiar with already). Previous chapters have given you a glimpse of the origins of narcissism, a conceptual understanding of these challenging people, and a background in several fields of psychological science that inform a strategy for changing your relationship with the narcissist. This strategy typically involves four stages:

1. **Observation:** You observe the specific behaviors, reactions, and interactions that characterize the relationship between you and the narcissist.

2. **Assessment:** Your observations and insights allow you to assess the dynamics in your relationship more accurately and perhaps more dispassionately.

3. **Identification:** Your assessment enables you to name the schemas that provoke ineffective coping responses, and to recognize self-defeating patterns in both of you.

4. **Differentiation:** Your identification of the schemas and coping responses at play allow you to differentiate experiences driven by memory and temperament from the here-and-now moments, thus liberating an authentic, sturdy, and credible voice.

Four Stages of Transformation

You may find journaling a useful adjunct to this process—and in general. Journaling can be a very soothing activity. It can also offer a new perspective on dysfunctional interactions and provide a place where you can express your authentic voice, rehearsing for real-world interactions. During the four-stage process discussed here, it can help with differentiation, allowing you to see biased thoughts and emotions as they emerge on the page before you. An example of the four stages might look something like this:

1. **Observation:** You notice that in your relationship with the narcissist, you do most of the giving and he does most of the getting—especially getting his own way. You're prone to feeling guilty and apologizing for your limitations, while he's more likely to make excuses and blame others.

2. **Assessment:** You can see how the lack of balance in the relationship and its unfairness are linked to feelings of anxiety and despair. These feelings are connected to some of the earliest chapters in your life story.

3. **Identification:** With your new understanding of early maladaptive schemas, you can see how your emotional deprivation, defectiveness, self-sacrifice, and subjugation schemas are adding weight to these already painful feelings. You can see that you didn't receive adequate support and emotional nurturing as a child and you never felt good enough, causing you to build a fortress out of doing and giving. This helped you numb your need for love and approval—a longing you perceived as shameful. If you happen to know the childhood history of the narcissist in your life, or perhaps by using what you've gleaned from this book, you can probably connect the dots to see how his schemas fit within the predictable patterns of conflict and how they influence the choreography of his undesirable actions and reactions.

4. **Differentiation:** The art of knowing the difference between what was and what is, differentiation allows you to be in your mind and your body in the present. Armed with the knowledge of which schemas and coping patterns are involved in the dynamics of your relationship, you can lay down your well-worn weaponry. You recognize that you are no longer a powerless child, but

rather a competent, wise, and lovable adult who can take a stand without defending or giving in.

Here's a simple example of how your authentic, sturdy, and credible voice might sound when negotiating with your partner about changing a well-established routine: "I know you enjoy watching your favorite TV shows on Thursday night. It also happens to be the one weeknight that we could possibly do something fun together, such as have a date night. Could we perhaps do that once or twice a month? You could record your programs on those nights. We often end up arguing about Thursday night activities, and I always end up giving in. I'd really appreciate it if we could agree on a compromise. I haven't been aware of how much I've struggled with and resented this, and how much I need your consideration and flexibility as well."

Here's another example, using an interaction with a supervisor: "It's not very easy for me to say this because I'm aware of my long-standing tendency to do what I'm told, even if I don't agree or if I have another, possibly better solution. Sometimes I'm overly invested in your approval of me. However, I want to propose that we improve our marketing efforts in this way... I also think that you and I should have regularly scheduled meetings to measure the progress on this project. The current process leaves me feeling invisible and sometimes unfairly criticized, even though I'm sure that isn't your intention."

Given your past experiences, you may wonder (or suddenly notice your mouth gaping at the thought of this proposal) whether such an approach will actually work. Here's another example that proves it can. A client named Carolyn married a narcissistic man, Damian, and inherited his narcissistic seventeen-year-old daughter, Lucy—Daddy's prideful princess. During her visits, Lucy could woo her father into giving her whatever she wanted and letting her off any hook. There were no rules or consequences, even when Lucy disrespected Carolyn, borrowed her things without asking, or sabotaged Carolyn and Damian's plans for a night out. Lucy never showed any appreciation, rarely cooperated, and felt no qualms about racking up credit card charges.

Carolyn felt helpless—not surprising—given Damian's harsh decree: "My daughter, my rules, period." Despite Carolyn's fear of another failed marriage, she worked up enough courage to advocate for herself and told Damian that if things didn't change, she was leaving. Although Carolyn didn't expect it at the time, this new, assertive approach created the leverage needed for change. After several bouts of typical behavior, in which Damian proclaimed, "Who cares! Go right ahead and leave," he actually agreed to enter therapy and work on these issues with Carolyn and Lucy. Carolyn, now in her healthy adult mode and no longer at the mercy of her abandonment and shame schemas, will be better able to thoughtfully choose whether to stay in this marriage.

Cues and Clues: Knowing Why You Get Triggered

The past informs the present, awakening the mind's automatic mechanisms for identifying threatening conditions and steering us to safety. In chapter 3, you learned about the coping responses Francine, Beth, and Bill exhibited when their early maladaptive schemas were triggered by Louis's challenging behaviors. With time and guidance, each of them learned to identify the uncomfortable physical and mental sensations that arose. Each learned to link this familiar distress to their relevant schemas. They soon noticed that the familiarity of sensations triggering their schemas seemed to automatically drive their correspondingly familiar, though ineffective, responses.

exercise: Why the Narcissist Triggers You

If you haven't already identified your own schemas, go back to chapter 2, review the list again, and look for schemas that most accurately represent the themes of your life. Keep in mind that early maladaptive schemas have roots in your childhood or adolescence. And, though it may be dormant throughout much of your life, you feel it acutely as you read about it now. Go ahead and list your schemas on a piece of paper.

With an awareness of your schemas firmly in mind, proceed with the following exercise. Because it involves a guided visualization, you'll need to read through it first to familiarize yourself with the steps before actually doing them.

1. Find a quiet place where you won't be interrupted and sit comfortably. Close your eyes for a moment. Try to recall a painful childhood memory involving one of your caregivers, a sibling, a teacher, or someone from your peer group. Assign a part of you to act as a sentry—remaining keenly watchful of your feet firmly planted on the ground, safely anchored to this moment, here and now—so that you can permit yourself to gently look back and notice the thoughts, feelings, and sensations that emerge as you call up this difficult event. What happened during this painful event? How did you deal with it? Can you recall what you wish had happened at that time? What were your deepest longings? If recalling the experience becomes difficult or painful, remind yourself that you are only remembering. Affirm to yourself that you had rights and needs that mattered.

2. Take a slow, deep breath in and then slowly exhale. Blank out the images of that past event but continue to hold on to the thoughts, emotions, and sensations that fill your mind and body. Keep them with you, allowing your soft and gentle breath to caress any painful associations etched on the walls of your mind.

3. Now call up a picture of the narcissist in your life. See if you can zoom in on a difficult, upsetting, or annoying encounter—past or potential. Make the image as vivid as possible within your mind. Pay attention to the thoughts, emotions, and physical sensations that resonate as this charged scenario unfolds within you. If you could control the outcome, what do you wish would happen? What are your deepest longings? Affirm to yourself that you have rights and needs that matter.

4. Take a couple of slow, gentle breaths, in and out, then open your eyes and give yourself a moment to become fully reengaged

with your surroundings. Say thank you to the part of you that kept you safely grounded so that you could make the journey.

After you complete the practice, compare the thoughts, emotions, and physical sensations associated with the first image—your memory from childhood—with those of the second. Was there a shift, or were they consistent? The difference indicates the degree to which your capacity to observe, assess, identify, and differentiate has emerged. Turning your awareness to your internal experience during these scenarios also allows you to measure the strength of your schemas and how entrenched your maladaptive coping modes are.

When you compare your internal experience in these two scenarios, do you see any patterns? How have your longings changed since that childhood experience, if at all? What do you continue to long for? What keeps you from getting those desires met? There's a lot to consider here. You may wish to take some time to write about your thoughts and feelings to help you sort through your emotions. Doing so may also be useful in the future, allowing you to gauge your progress.

Finally, review the list of your schemas one more time. Do you feel reasonably confident that you've accurately identified those most pertinent to your life story—those that may be implicitly interfering with you finding your voice? If so, good for you. If not, don't worry. This is a complex task, and you may have multiple layers of history and behavioral patterns to unfold. Read on; there is much more ahead that will assist you in your discovery.

Making Sense of Our Senses: Messages from the Brain and Body

As you now know, sometimes your schemas will be triggered (often outside of your awareness), activating less-than-impressive responses as your soldiers of self-preservation report for duty. There are also plenty of times when you successfully respond to the challenges of your life with wise restraint or a clever riposte, as needed. If this is seldom possible when dealing with the narcissist in your life, you're not alone; these challenging folks seem to have a knack for triggering people's schemas in the strongest form. Perhaps why this is the case for you is clearer now that you've begun to uncover your private collection of life themes and corresponding coping styles. Though these coping styles may not have served you well, they can provide valuable clues about your cognitive and sensory system and, as such, are essential guideposts along the way to healthy liberation.

Bring to mind the potent sensations you experienced in the previous exercise while recalling a painful memory. The sensations in your mind and body swelled and took on a sense of powerlessness entirely out of proportion with the reality of the current situation in which you sat quietly alone. Such is the sway of schemas; they are woven into your sensory system and can initiate forceful and intense sensations when they are triggered.

The sensory system includes your muscles, nervous system, and viscera. When your schemas are triggered, you may notice some combination of the following physical sensations:

- Increased heart rate

- Elevated blood pressure

- Increased skin temperature

- Faster breathing rate

- A damp brow or palms

- A queasy or achy feeling in your stomach

- Tightness or a lump in your throat

- Dry mouth

- Quivering lips

- Tingling in your hands, feet, or legs

- A sudden stiffness in your neck, back, or joints

- Dizziness

- Welling of tears

- Sleepiness

- Pain or numbness in parts of your body

- Tension in your muscles

- Your mind going blank

- A heightening or dulling of your senses: sound, smell, visual recognition, taste, or touch

Why is this relevant? Because schemas, in conspiracy with your sensory system, send messages from the body to the brain and vice versa, setting off alarms to arouse self-protective action. The problem is that the brain can be fooled. It can't easily differentiate between a stomachache brought on by a virus and one brought on by a marathon melee with the narcissist. And further, it is prone to associating either of these with those unforgettable stomachaches in first grade at parochial school, when you were terrorized by the threat of burning in the fires of hell if your knee socks were crinkly, thus tilling the soil for your mistrust schema.

Without mindful attunement to your inner state and structure, subtle and not-so-subtle sensory stimuli can leave you feeling suspicious and on edge anytime you feel queasy. If, on the other hand, you can make sense of the uneasy feeling in your stomach, attributing it to a definite physical cause (*I have a nauseous feeling because I caught the bug that everyone in my office has, not because danger lurks ahead*), you might be able to set aside doubt and simply rest. Alternatively, you might start to see a pattern of nonphysical causes (*I have a nauseous feeling every time I get into it with my coworker Sherry because I wind up feeling like Sister Joseph Marie is about to toss me down the chute to hell without sunscreen*), in which case you might be able to garner your courage and stand up to Sherry with sturdiness and conviction. To be successful in this, you must invite your brain to download a new mantra: *That was then, and this is now.* Chapter 5 will give you many tools for making the distinction and living by that mantra.

exercise: Anticipating the Glitches and Activating Your Radar

Now that you've learned about the insidious ways in which schemas can activate painful emotions and distressing physical sensations, you're probably eager to learn how to short-circuit this response. Building on the previous exercise, this one also uses a visualization of a difficult encounter with your narcissist. Here, you'll begin to practice new awareness skills in the relative comfort and safety of your own mind, rather than one-on-one with the narcissist. You'll also gain some experience in using a positive and compassionate inner dialogue to place your schemas in perspective.

1.   Think about your next encounter with the narcissist. When and where will it occur? What will the circumstances of this meeting be?

2.   Think about all the possible interpersonal challenges that might arise during this encounter.

3.   Consider all that you can possibly predict about how you're likely to feel, given the importance of what brings you together, your typical level of sensitivity in such situations, and historical precedents in this type of situation. Consider everything from peripheral distractions to the worst-case scenario.

4.   Bring your attention to the sensations in your body and the thoughts moving through your mind. Point the radar of your awareness to your most vulnerable areas of sensitivity—those deep red thunderstorms embedded in the rainy background.

5.   If your senses could talk, what would they be saying? For example, if you have a defectiveness schema combined with a punitive coping mode, the tightness in your neck might say, *You're such a wimp; you can't even defend yourself.* Look at the sensations you're experiencing and try to identify what they're saying to you.

6.   Allow your wise and compassionate inner voice to engage those sensations in a dialogue. For example, you might say, *I was often made to feel that I wasn't good enough when I was young, but*

that just wasn't true. I was only a child. I had no capacity to stand up for myself then. I was young and scared. What I'm experiencing now is the resonant replay of that schema. But I have choices right now. I don't have to tolerate being treated this way by anyone anymore.

7. Notice how the sensations triggered by your imaginary encounter with the narcissist begin to slowly make their exit. If you can't come up with words to refute your schema, you might ask a friend, loved one, therapist, or anyone who really knows you to help you compose an authentic message that reflects your inner truth.

Having activated your internal radar, you can now scan your internal world for distorting schemas, those nemeses of truth. Later in the chapter, you'll learn more communication skills and get more chances to rehearse for successful interactions with the narcissist in your life.

Charmed and Disarmed

As you may recall, the narcissist has the unremitting power to intoxicate your senses with his charm and beguiling wit. He can make you feel special and chosen with his attention. And just as you begin to swoon, you find yourself squinting in the dark for the exit sign. He will get you the best seat in the house for his swaggering performance. In return, you're expected to hold the spotlight steadily upon him, nod affirmatively during his orations, laugh on cue, never appear bored, applaud loudly and frequently, and never, ever expect to share the stage.

Bait and Switch Maneuvers

The narcissist's charm is an enticing lure. It's also an effective tool for keeping you from examining the potential costs of the relationship until you're hooked. Let's take a look at some specific examples of the subtle but classic bait and switch maneuvers narcissists use. This might help you gain a clearer perspective on the dynamic in your own relationship with a narcissist.

The vanishing act. After promising you his undying attention, the narcissist becomes unavailable. With no acknowledgment or contrition, he accuses you of being selfish and needy when you feel upset about it.

The setup. Having solicited your input with enthusiasm, the narcissist proceeds to assassinate your response and annihilate your self-esteem with demeaning criticisms.

Dr. Jekyll and Mr. Hyde. Seizing the opportunity to be your hero, the narcissist will be abundantly protective when others are unfair to you. But he will have no compunction about cutting you to the quick with his harsh and lordly tones if you dare to interrupt him or question his opinions or actions, especially when he is the perpetrator of your pain.

Adding insult to injury. The narcissist will show up unexpectedly with a truckload of roses to make you feel disposed to forgive his behavior. You reciprocate with acts of love and appreciation, but nothing is ever enough for the chasm of insatiability, leaving you grinding your teeth between guilt and exasperation. Eventually, it's all about him again.

Devil's advocate. Like the president of a debate club, the narcissist invites you into a conversation that quickly becomes either a drawn-out soliloquy or an argument. No matter what your response—ignoring him, fighting back, pleading, or even giving in—he is impervious.

Do any of these maneuvers sound familiar? If all of them do, don't despair. Many of my clients report that all five are often relevant. Remember, the narcissist maintains very high, unrelenting standards for himself, and for those who orbit his stellar magnificence. As you have also learned, narcissists have an extremely high need for recognition, approval, control, victory, and acknowledgment. They have these needs because of a fierce inner current of shame, emotional loneliness, and mistrust. Self-righteous behavior is merely a plug in the emotional dam.

Typical Emotional Responses

Clearly, the narcissist doesn't feel bound to play by the same rules as the rest of us. These bait and switch maneuvers are unfair, and, worse, the narcissist's personality doesn't allow for calling the behavior into question or negotiating a solution. In the absence of fair communication and negotiation, each of the maneuvers tends to elicit a specific response.

Insecurity. When the narcissist is performing his vanishing act, the instability of his mood and unreliability of his presence may leave you feeling alone and insecure. This feeling may harken back to memories of unstable relationships during your early life.

Intimidation. The setup maneuver can be downright intimidating, like being gently coaxed to dip your toe into piranha-infested water. This maneuver can often mimic childhood scenarios, such as your parent encouraging you to choose something for dinner and then criticizing your choice. In response, you learned how to read between the lines to find the "right" answer, even if it wasn't necessarily your own.

Resentment. When the narcissist transforms from Dr. Jekyll into the odious Mr. Hyde, you become resentful of his superiority, selfishness, and inability to compromise, especially if only fifteen minutes ago he was heroically defending you. Suddenly his support doesn't feel like it was about you at all. This can feel like those rare times when your mother called you from your room to join her at the table with her friends. It was nice to feel included and wanted, but within moments you realized it was just a ploy so she could bask in everyone's oohs and aahs over what a beautiful job she'd done with you. Once again, you were left dutifully holding the spotlight on her "mother of the year" performance.

Provocation. How does the narcissist manage to be so charming when heaping insult atop injury? And why do you fall for it every time? You're not foolish. It feels good to be cared for and treated kindly. You go out on a limb to be appreciative of the narcissist's gallantry, only to find that the charming prince you've kissed is really a frog. You feel provoked because you were once again captured by the mini-moments of magic and forced to pay the price. This may be reminiscent of a dynamic with your parents; perhaps you savored the all-too-rare loving attention a narcissistic mother showered on you when you were ill, only to be guilt-tripped because she lost sleep while taking care of you.

Powerlessness. The devil's advocate maneuver is primarily a way of elevating whatever the narcissist is orating about, leaving you feeling powerless and weary. You feel like it's a no-win situation; if you don't concede, he'll keep you up all night making his point and enjoying his own voice. This can sometimes feel like the powerlessness of being a child, especially if you learned to subjugate your voice to a parent or caregiver who wanted you to keep your ideas and opinions to yourself and respect her point of view as sacrosanct.

You have earned the right to be frustrated, upset, distressed, and downright angry about the mistreatment you suffer in this relationship with a narcissist. But you are no longer powerless. You do matter, you are loveable, and your thoughts and opinions and wishes and dreams are meaningful. Remember—that was then, and this is now.

In all the scenarios mentioned, you are primed to protect yourself but end up feeling provoked, insecure, intimidated, resentful, or powerless—ironically, quite unprotected.

Why? To understand this, we need to revisit how the brain works. When confronted by a grizzly bear, your mechanisms for survival are limited. You may try to run from the bear, try to fight him off, or just stand there, frozen in fear—typical fight, flight, or freeze responses. In schema therapy, we refer to these survival mechanisms as counterattack, avoidance, and surrender. For some people, the response often depends on the nature of the threat. For others, the response to any threat may always be the same.

The Low Road

In conversations with Dan Siegel, he helped me understand that when the brain senses a threat, the lower subcortical portions (the brain stem and limbic areas) become activated. Once the assessment of a threat is received by the brain, messages are transmitted to the body to create distress and ready you for action. Part of the response involves a discharge of excitatory hormones, such as adrenaline. This all occurs very rapidly. This hardwired system engages in a fight, flight, or freeze response that is invaluable for survival for most animals (including humans) when confronting a truly dangerous or life-threatening situation.

Dan Siegel has proposed what he calls a "low road" of function in which a state of threat can sometimes shut off the higher functions of the prefrontal cortex. The prefrontal area serves as the executive officer of your brain, and helps soothe your mind, regulate your body, reason, and reflect on what's going on—all functions that are lost on the low road. Without prefrontal reflection, you might not be able to recognize that a bump in the night is hot water in the pipes and not an intruder. Siegel's work offers a way to both understand and gain control over these low road experiences in our lives (Siegel 2001, 2007; Siegel and Hartzell 2004).

Interacting with the narcissist can sometimes activate both a perception of threat and immersion in the low road. But with reflection, you can interact with a narcissist without engaging in his dance. Instead of experiencing palpitations, headaches, and a dry mouth when the narcissist is close by, you might actually be able to show up with a confident internal self-advocate, a sense of worth, and a strong, authentic voice.

Beyond Fight, Flight, or Freeze

Achieving effective results in your interactions with a narcissist requires modifications to the choreography of your survival system. To help you adjust your internal alarms, let's take a look at some typical fight, flight, and freeze responses, how these responses can be modified, and how to most effectively communicate from this new stance.

Counterattack (the fight response). If you're prone to fighting back when you feel stonewalled, punished, or verbally attacked, your inner dialogue is one of *I'll show you*. This, of course, usually results in a wearying battle, a heightened verbal onslaught, or increased aggression or withdrawal from your opponent.

- **Modification:** Fighters need not give up the fight. You just need to stand up for yourself without attacking. For example, instead of *I'll show you*, your inner dialogue can become *I have rights too*.

- **Communication:** Your new approach might sound like this: "Though it probably isn't your intention, I feel devalued by your actions and words. I won't tolerate being disrespected. If you're uncomfortable with me, you can tell me without putting me down or ignoring me. You have rights, and so do I. I'd appreciate it if you could speak to me with more consideration, and I will do the same for you." You can also enlist the "narrator" voice—one that describes the rising anger but also knows better where that dance always leads: "I am feeling so angry inside and I know that if I engage you now, we will wind up dancing the same dysfunctional dance yet again. I am not willing to do that anymore." You exit the room to take time to breathe, regulate your system, and prepare a confrontation that will come from the "high road."

Avoidance (the flight response). If you're prone to running away when things are difficult, your inner dialogue is one of *See ya later*. But the more you avoid, the more your narcissistic opponent pursues, demands, and persists. You end up feeling cornered, incapacitated, and abandoned by your own voice.

- **Modification:** If you are someone who needs distance from disquieting exchanges, that's okay. But to resolve a conflict, you need to eventually return. Your inner dialogue might go from *See ya later* to *I need a time-out*.

- **Communication:** Consider this approach: "I know this issue is very important to you. It's also important to me, but I'm feeling flooded right now. In the spirit of protecting myself and this relationship, I need some time alone to regroup and gather my thoughts so our conversation might be productive. Perhaps you could benefit from it too."

Surrender (the freeze response). If you're prone to becoming immobilized in interactions that feel threatening, your only means of releasing yourself from the narcissist's sticky grip is to give in, take the blame, and agree. Your inner dialogue is one of *You're right; it's all my fault*. Unfortunately, this often results in further controlling behaviors and criticism for your fragile and flawed disposition.

- **Modification:** If you have a reflexive freeze response, you may find a rehearsed script helpful. Your inner dialogue may go from *It's all my fault* to *I may not be perfect, but it's not all my fault*.

- **Communication:** Your new approach might sound like this: "It seems that you're upset with me, and when I sense that, I have a tendency to give up and give in. I know this makes you more upset, but that isn't my intention. I get triggered by these exchanges, but I'm working to strengthen my confidence. I'd appreciate it if you could be more thoughtful toward me. You have responsibilities in this relationship too."

Conclusion

You've seen how your life experiences and biological makeup account for the personally relevant schemas and reactions that become obstacles to effectively caring for yourself and weathering painful encounters with the narcissist. You've practiced activating your inner radar to anticipate when you might fall prey to old habits, and you've begun to learn how to attend to sensory information. Although humans are equipped with reflexive responses for survival, we're also extraordinarily flexible creatures. You've started to see how adapting your internal dialogues and adopting new approaches to communication can lead to a greater sense of self-advocacy and authenticity in difficult relationships, and also influence change.

Chapter 5 will further hone your skills in attending to sensory information. You'll learn the value of mindful attention in building new habits and enhancing flexibility in communication. You'll also continue to compose new scripts for managing interpersonal transactions with a genuine voice.

Paying Attention:
Facing Difficult Encounters with a Narcissist

Everything that we see is a shadow cast by that which we do not see.

—Martin Luther King Jr.

S o far, you've devoted time and effort to making sense of your life, examining your life themes, and understanding how your past contributes to your sometimes luminous and other times dusky emotional life. You've investigated the links between your experiences, inclinations, and schemas. You have a sense of why dealing with a narcissist is particularly difficult, as well as why you might be drawn to these people. You can anticipate and recognize your triggers, and have a new set of skills for understanding yourself and the narcissist, and for communicating more effectively and authentically.

The next step is to fully ground yourself in the moment. You know the expression "in one ear and out the other," which is a great example of our Teflon-coated brains. Sometimes things just slide right out of awareness. This can be liberating, allowing us to let go of cacophonous orchestrations of the mind. So, when Ms. Knows-It-All-and-Does-No-Wrong gets in your face with a careless, painful comment about your life or goes off about how wonderful she is (poorly disguised by sophomoric modesty), you access the Teflon-coated element of your brain, press your internal "mute" button, power off your schemas, and take a deep breath. You masterfully hold the narcissist accountable, or you move on. Where your "noisy" mind would have had you feeling flustered, furious, self-doubtful, or helpless, your distress now slides away like a fluffy omelet departing a well-coated pan.

Breaking Free from Your Mechanical Habits

A fully felt sense of who you are, and why, is a powerful tool. But to really be effective, you'll need to develop some supporting skills, chiefly the ability to identify unhealthy habits and when you engage in them. This is key to new ways of responding to and interacting with the narcissist in your life.

As a human, you're predisposed to seek that which is familiar and respond with learned, developed, and innate behaviors. And while some of these habits are healthy and adaptive, others hold you hostage in emotionally and physically painful schema activations. Therefore, it is essential to have a clear mental picture of your inner life—particularly the vulnerable parts—and true compassion for yourself. This will allow you to shift your focus and responses when you feel vulnerable. Instead of coping with the old messages like *I'm unlovable, No one could ever meet my needs, I have no rights, It's my responsibility to make other people happy*, you can shift to more realistic assessments, freeing you from these long-held and biased themes. Once you've deconstructed and revised these damaging thought patterns, keep your new, more equitable reality at hand to ward off schemas and better manage the conditions that trigger them, particularly being with narcissistic people.

So how do you steer clear of that entrapment? Memory is a powerful force, and with memory come schemas to manage. But if your newly wise and loving internal voice is an attentive and reasonable advocate, you'll have far fewer triggering moments, and when you are triggered, it will be less intense. That is, perhaps, as good as it gets. And it isn't too bad—especially since you can't be attentive 24/7. At times, you may slip into old habits, demanding to be heard, burying your head in your pillow, or numbly staring at the walls around you. But remember, it's only a slip, not an indication that you are inherently flawed or doomed to failure. You'll discover that you can hoist yourself out of that darkness and back into the present. The imagination is also a powerful resource, one that integrates with memory and allows us to breathe in the possibilities that come with choosing our path. When we fully imagine ourselves as rightful, worthy, and loveable souls, we can also imagine ourselves as powerful, vital self-advocates.

Let's say, for example, you encounter Mr. Life-of-the-Party-Can't-Even-Remember-Your-Name. You slip into your intimidated and anxious mode (*I have nothing to contribute, so I'll just keep my thoughts to myself*) and your stomach aches. This is your cue. Recognize this sensation and the beliefs attached to it. Take a few moments to direct a kind focus on your inner world, perhaps with a gentle, discreet stretch or a few easy breaths, and tune in to the words of your internal advocate—the inner voice that can tell you the truth when you slip. Recall that you're fine, and that your reaction is simply the old, nagging stuff of memory. Remember that you have rights and opinions, and that you're entitled to have a good time. Having soothed your internal world, you can wisely maneuver yourself to limit your encounters with Mr. Omni Glorious, and when in his presence, you can maintain your voice and your integrity.

One of my clients came up with a clever metaphor while working on covert narcissism and his eating habits. We were investigating his approval-seeking tendencies and the upset he felt around his very popular (and also narcissistic) colleague Joe: "Joe is the cheeseburger that I really *want*. If he would only accept me into his inner circle, then I would feel I was truly special. But I know that what I really *need*, and actually enjoy, is the chicken wrap—because I'm already special, and caring for myself means bringing healthier people into my life. My mom didn't know how to take care of me and make me feel loved. I want Joe to accept me because my schema has me feeling that I'm not good enough, that I need to be extraordinary and friends with popular guys in order to truly matter. Joe is an elixir for my pain, but the truth is, we have nothing in common, so the best he could ever be is a prop in my life. I don't need props. I need friends."

The Power of Mindful Awareness

To see yourself clearly and avoid becoming trapped by your schemas and old habits, it's important to develop mindful awareness. You got a taste of this in the previous chapter. Now, we'll develop this skill further. Simply put, mindful awareness means paying attention, or being attuned, to your experience—both external and internal. You intentionally initiate your sensory system and point your awareness wherever you choose. As my friend Laura Fortgang, a talented author and acclaimed professional life coach, describes it, "Being mindful means being aware of everything and certain of nothing." I love this because certainty eclipses possibility. The possibility of seeing and feeling through a new lens is the harvest of the flexible mind. With awareness and flexibility, you enlist the possibility of seeing the depth, color, and movement of the world. For example, consider the ocean. With mindful attention, you can hear the surf with robust dimensionality, feel the warm mist and the radiant sun on your face, and even taste the salt tang of the air. Being fully attuned to your senses allows you to engage in a multifaceted experience of the present moment.

The Importance of Practice

Developing a mindfully fit brain requires regular practice. Think about riding a bike or driving a car. Before you were able to take in the scenery, you had to think carefully about your position, posture, steering, speed, and visual cues.

Years ago, a friend agreed to teach me how to drive a stick shift. He said I should tackle the tough stuff right from the start, so we started on a steep incline during rush hour. Though I was already an experienced driver, I felt my sweaty palms clenching the wheel, my back stiff, and my eyes darting to the vehicle behind me in the rearview mirror. My heart pounded in time with the silent refrain: *Left foot engage clutch. Release brake. Accelerate gas pedal with right foot. Gently remove left foot from clutch. Don't wreck your friend's new car.*

Developing this new skill involved intense concentration and effort. But soon, I found myself driving my newly purchased stick-shift automobile uphill in traffic while listening to the radio, taking in the scenery, and thinking about my upcoming midterm exam. In that moment, I didn't need to focus on the mechanics of driving anymore, at least not as much as before. Driving stick had now become a memory-accessible, choreographed set of movements. Of course, if you drive regularly, you are enrolled in ongoing practice—practice that reinforces your skill set.

You might be able to pluck a similar experience from your own memories. Try this:

1. Recall the first time you learned something that required your complete focus and attention.

2. See how many of your senses you can engage as you remember that experience: how it felt, looked, sounded, smelled, and tasted, along with your thoughts and emotions at the very beginning.

3. How long was it before you no longer needed to pay such concentrated attention—until there appeared to be an opening for other awareness?

If your memory is of artistic or athletic pursuits—tennis, for example—you may be thinking that you must always focus if you want to play well. But recall the difference between your first time on the court and the first time you were able to focus on both hitting the ball and anticipating your opponent's next move.

We've all heard the saying "Practice makes perfect." I don't know about perfect, but practice is the key to getting information or behaviors to stick to memory. Whether it's practicing your backhand stroke, the piano, or not cowering before an intimidating individual, you are immersed in the intentional act of doing something again and again with several goals in mind:

- Learning new habits

- Unlearning undesirable habits

- Performing well enough or better

- Making all this stick to memory and perhaps developing a sense of mastery

How Mindfulness Helps You Interact with the Narcissist

In dealing with narcissists, it's important to practice the art of paying attention. For example, if you're mindfully aware of your shoulders slumped with resignation while approaching the narcissist, you're more likely to engage the possibility of positive change. You might notice that your posture arises from anticipating the usual defeat. From this moment of clarity, you choose to adopt a chin-up, shoulders-back position of strength and confidence, and angle your awareness toward the other person's face, hands, and physical being, reminding yourself that he is just another imperfect human. With your body and mind well attuned, and with a more realistic assessment of the situation, you are unburdened of the shoulds, the musts, and the schemas. You not only know that you're okay, you also feel it.

Awareness fosters discovery, which in turn fosters freedom and responsibility for how you show up in the world. Instead of showing the narcissist your guilt-ridden, subjugated, or powerless self, you can be anchored in your authentic, healthy, and grown-up self. Armed with the ownership of your present moment and connected with a wise understanding of the narcissist's underlying shame and defectiveness, you'll have the confidence to tactfully confront him when he crosses the line. By awakening to your automatic reactions, you can recognize several important things:

- Sudden discomfort may be a sign of schema activation.

- The thoughts and feelings activated by your memories may not have any bearing on the present situation.

- You have choices in the present moment.

- You have nothing to prove and no need to hide.

- You have rights too.

As you develop a mindful brain, you can flex your thoughts, beliefs, and predictions like muscles honed by careful training and exercise. And just as in developing muscles, becoming grounded in the present moment requires regular practice, even if it's sometimes accompanied by pain. With so much to gain from developing mindfulness, you're probably eager to get started. The following exercise details a simple practice for keeping your mind attuned.

exercise: Engaging Your Mindful Brain

As discussed, practice is crucial to developing new skills. Commit to carving out five minutes twice a day to engage in the following practice. For a printable version of this exercise that you can carry with you, go to www.new harbinger.com/47704. (See back of book for more information.) Of course, adding more time to each practice will make your experience more robust and will help to lock in your newly developed awareness skills. You can do this practice almost anywhere as long as you aren't likely to be interrupted by someone talking to you.

Closing your eyes promotes a deeper and more profound rendezvous with your senses, but keeping them open if you need to is also fine. Read through the instructions several times to familiarize yourself with the process. Consider making a recording of the instructions to use until your mindfulness practice becomes second nature. As you practice, engage all your senses.

1. Direct your attention to your breath, and without forcing anything, just maintain the natural pace of your breath and focus on each of the following aspects in turn:

   - With the first breath, notice the rise and fall of your abdomen.

   - With the second breath, tune in to the expansion and contraction of your lungs.

   - With the third breath, feel the cool air coming through your nostrils as you breathe in, and sense the warmth of the air you exhale.

2. Repeat the above process three times, noticing the rise and fall of your abdomen, your lungs expanding and contracting, and the temperature of the air as you inhale and exhale.

3. If your eyes are open, visually notice the space you're occupying. If they're closed, conjure up a memory of this space. Label what you see: the color, size, shape, dimension, and movement of whatever surrounds you.

4. Notice the sounds in your environment. Allow them to enter your auditory awareness precisely and without judgment. Label each one, from the roaring lyrics of the lawnmower pressing through your window to the rambling medley of children's voices in play and even to the most subtle sounds: the whistle of the air ventilation duct, the tiny tick of the clock, or the faint hum coming from your laptop sitting on your desk.

5. Invite your nasal passages to join you in your practice, making sense out of scents in the air.

6. Point the needle of your compass of awareness to your tongue. As you take a slow breath in and then release it, notice and label any tastes in your mouth.

7. Direct your attention toward the sensations of anything that you are physically in contact with. Notice your clothing against your skin, a breeze brushing your face, the texture of the surface or firmness of the cushion you're sitting on, the feeling of the ground beneath your feet or the sand between your toes.

8. Turn your attention to your internal world, the world under your skin. If possible, engage in a few simple stretches accompanied by nice, full breaths. Starting with the crown of your head, slowly scan your entire body from top to bottom. Take notice of sensations in your muscles and viscera: energy, fatigue, tightness, tingling, soreness, numbness, strength, queasiness, or weakness, for example. Just notice. Be aware of emotional responses emerging within. You may notice that your inner sensations emit a resonance of sadness, fear, or anger. Just notice this, label it, and allow your attention to rest upon it quietly, observing without appraisal.

Try to maintain a stance of openness and equanimity, meaning without predictions or predilections crowding your mind. Your thoughts *will* try to seduce you away from your practice. When that happens, just notice them, label them, acknowledge them, and let them move on. If thoughts like *This is foolish. How could this possibly make a difference?* leak in, simply notice that you're having a thought and that this thought is a judgment. Tell yourself, *Okay, I got it*, then let it go and return to your practice.

If schema-driven thoughts invade (for example, *Nothing will ever help me get my needs met; I'm destined to be emotionally lonely and unfulfilled*), use the process of observing, assessing, identifying, and differentiating described in chapter 4. Observe that you're having a familiar thought and assess whether it might relate to an old life theme or schema. If so, identify or label it and acknowledge your understanding of where it comes from. (For example, *Okay, I got it. I know this is my emotional deprivation schema. It makes me feel like I'll never get my needs met.*) Differentiate it by saying, *But that was then, and this is now.* Then let it go and return to your practice.

Some thoughts, especially those associated with schemas, can be stubborn. Your breath is your grounding point. It gently returns you to your practice when you become swept away by the undertow of your thoughts. When you find yourself distracted, return your attention to your breathing, noticing the rise and fall of your abdomen, your lungs expanding and contracting, and the temperature of the air as you inhale and exhale.

Somatic Experiencing

We can also use somatic experiencing (body work) strategies to settle the mind and body in preparation for and dealing with the aftermath of challenging interactions with the narcissist. For example, notice where the discomfort sits in your body. It may have claimed multiple places—for example, your back, neck, or a quickened pulse. Zoom in on these areas of distress and just notice them. Now look around your body for a spot that is completely calm, unbothered, peaceful—perhaps your pinky finger. Take your full attention to that pinky (or other quiet place in your body) and just rest yourself there for a few moments. Absorb the calm, quiet, and peacefulness of your pinky, for example. Enjoy taking refuge in these moments. Gently swing your attention back to the discomfort zones and notice their intensity, and then swing back to your pinky. Allow yourself some time to engage your quiet spot. Swing your attention back and forth like a seamless glider until there is calm throughout your body and quiet in your mind. You've regained your resilience and your sturdiness. Good for you!

The Rewards of Mindfulness

Creating a practice of intentional awareness, mindful discovery, and body work can unwrap many beautiful gifts. It also reveals the undesirable ones. Remember, memories are stored in the brain and in the body, and they can be released by infinite sensory stimuli. Fortunately, as your awareness becomes well-attuned, you can readily discern between truth and fiction, past and present. This is exactly what you need for taking on the most difficult people in your life with aplomb.

Illuminating the majesty of the brain, Dan Siegel explains that, in an attentive state, the brain is capable of reflective awareness, allowing you to differentiate your feelings, thoughts, and sensations, and also integrate them within the whole of your mind and body. Without mindful attention, you operate out of the default state of automatic mental activity. The brain is reactive, not necessarily receptive (Siegel 2007).

Of course, in our busy lives, it isn't possible to be in a state of attentive awareness all the time. To always be perfectly conscious would disable our necessary automatic functionality. Paying attention is a choice and a discipline. Just as paying attention to your body through conscious eating and exercise may reward you with good health, paying attention, on purpose, to your thoughts, feelings, and sensations potentially rewards you by alerting you to delightful moments worth capturing—and distortions worth discarding, especially when dealing with the narcissist in your life.

The Four Most Common Masks of the Narcissist and How to Deal with Them

Armed with an understanding of narcissism, a custom profile of the narcissist in your life, an inventory of your own schemas and coping styles, and your attentive and flexible brain, you're ready to move on to specific strategies for dealing with the four masks of the narcissist you're most likely to encounter: the show-off, the bully, the entitled one, and the addictive self-soother. Remember: It will take time, practice, and repetition to change these longstanding "dances." Your goal is threefold: (1) to effect positive changes, even small ones; (2) to bear witness to your own healthy inner advocate standing up for you, without doubt and reluctance; and (3) readying yourself to issue necessary limits and consequences.

The Show-Off

The show-off hungers for the adoration and envy of others. She may be overtly boastful or covertly charming and self-effacing. She suffers from a deep sense of invalidity and undesirability but may not be aware of it. If she can impress you, she can temporarily nourish her hunger and extinguish her shame. She seeks her approval in your applause. She appears to have little interest in you apart from the praise and admiration you offer.

With your steady grasp of the present moment, ignore her obvious solicitations and instead offer positive feedback for simple niceties. Let's say the narcissist is your friend Vanessa. Instead of saying, "Oh, Vanessa, I just don't know how you do it all. What an exceptional woman you are," you could place your emphasis on everyday things: "Vanessa, I appreciate that you made this lunch date for us. It's nice to be remembered." Focus on thoughtful, unadorned kindnesses instead of the extraordinary, supremely glossy actions she presents for your admiration. Even amid her outstanding achievements, you might ferret out a sliver of ordinariness and grant it some honest but modest recognition.

Say she's just been asked to chair the hospital's annual fund-raising gala—a social extravaganza. Following her blow-by-blow account of how they invited her based on her reputation, poise, and exemplary public relations skills, you could respond with, "How nice for you, Vanessa, to be a part of raising money for a good cause. Good luck with it."

You competently steered clear of the narcissist's traps and your "make-nice" schemas and didn't allow yourself to be blinded by her 24-karat ego. While you bask in your own clarity, know that your frank responses might even touch on Vanessa's longing to be accepted without having to prove herself.

The Bully

The bully has a rigid mistrust of people and their motives. He's fearful that others will try to control him, make a fool of him, or take advantage of him. He believes that no one could truly care about him, given his history of emotional voids and his deep sense of shame and inadequacy. He protects himself by being critical and controlling of others. To achieve his craved sense of importance and authority, he must ensure that you feel weak, lesser, powerless, and perhaps even stupid.

With your steady grasp of the present moment and new insights, you are confident and look the bully in the eye, ready to let him know how his words and actions make you feel. Let's say the narcissist is Brad, a colleague who's upset about your work. You might say, "You know, Brad, it's very difficult and, frankly, distressing when you speak to me in that tone, criticizing my work because it doesn't measure up to your expectations. I can appreciate that you're disappointed, perhaps frustrated, and I can accept that. However, you don't have to be mean about it. I don't think your intention is to hurt me, but you sometimes have a way of coming across as harshly critical. Not only is it upsetting, it's also not helpful or acceptable."

Or let's say you're at a party and Joe, your narcissistic significant other, just slipped into bully mode due to a perceived lack of attention from you. You might say, "Joe, I care about how you feel, and I certainly don't want you to feel ignored by me. I can understand that you may get upset when I'm distracted and that you'd like me to be more attentive. It's your responsibility to tell me that, not curse at me or call me names. It's really tough to care about you or your feelings when you do this. It isn't helpful to our relationship, and it simply isn't okay with me anymore."

In these scenarios, you've bypassed your former inclination to give in, apologize, counterattack, or run away and cry. Wrapped in the comforting embrace of your sturdy inner advocate, you're readied with courage and integrity.

The Entitled One

The entitled one feels that she can make up her own rules and should be able to have whatever she wants when she wants it. She behaves as if she is superior and deserves to be treated differently. She doesn't subscribe to the sentiment of give-and-take. She has trouble hearing "no" and never appears to feel any remorse for her often pushy and demanding actions. She isn't interested in the feelings of others and can't appreciate or comprehend the value of empathy.

With your steady grasp of the present moment, you gently emerge from the heat rising in your face, take a breath, steady your nerves, and proceed to let her know the real deal. Let's say the narcissist is your friend Leanne, who's joining you for dinner. As usual, she arrived thirty-five minutes late without calling. The restaurant has a policy that you can't be seated until the entire party has arrived, so you've been waiting at the bar, watching the tables fill. Leanne struts in with no apology and no explanation, and when she's told there will be a wait for a table, she angrily expresses her annoyance to the manager. You are embarrassed by the loud and self-righteous scene she's making and upset by her total lack of respect for you and the value of your time.

This isn't the first time you've found yourself wishing to be invisible during one of Leanne's entitled tirades. Typically, you stand back and smile shyly and apologetically for her rude and embarrassing behavior, then roll your eyes and think, *Oh well, this is who she is.* But this time you call her aside and say, "Leanne, this is uncomfortable and embarrassing.

It's disappointing that you don't seem to have regard for my feelings. You act as if it's perfectly okay to do as you please, even when it has a negative impact on me. I know that you're accustomed to taking charge and getting your way, and you take pride in that. It's great to have that kind of savvy in certain situations. But it isn't okay for you to dismiss my rights and my feelings. I know that you may be too upset to talk about this right now, and I suggest that we postpone our dinner. I'm open to talking about this after you've had a chance to calm down."

Bravo. No cowering, no making excuses for her, no letting her off the hook again.

The Addictive Self-Soother

The addictive self-soother is in a state of unknowing avoidance. The intolerable discomfort associated with his loneliness, shame, and disconnection when the spotlight isn't on him sends him hiding beneath the floorboards once again. He may be engrossed in workaholism, drinking binges, spending marathons, or voracious internet surfing. He may indulge in yet another tiring oration—not necessarily because he's seeking attention, but to avoid feeling the throbbing pulse of his aloneness and fragility. You may go knocking, but he doesn't come out. He can't risk being seen au naturel, with all of his emotions, needs, and longings revealed. You're expected to pander to his selective emotional departures and not request his presence, regardless of the emotional costs to you.

Steadily grasping the present, you remind yourself that he doesn't don this mask on purpose, and that it isn't your fault. You act with healthy entitlement and advocacy for yourself, especially if this is a meaningful relationship. Let's say the narcissist is your husband, Al, and he's deeply entrenched in one of his workaholic episodes. You proceed to thoughtfully confront him, saying, "I know how important your work is to you, Al, and I appreciate how your ambition and dedication have provided us with financial security and lovely opportunities. But I miss you, and I'm concerned that you might be pushing harder than necessary. It's difficult for me to sit back and watch without sharing my concern and sense of loss with you. I'd like to talk about it and see if we can come up with a compromise. Please don't dismiss me or say that I just don't get it. This is really important to me. If we can't come up with a solution that satisfies both of our needs, I want to seek professional help."

No longer tossing in the towel or apologizing for your supposed ignorance about his career, you firmly but thoughtfully reach in to pull him from the darkness of the lonely place he inhabits.

Conclusion

Greetings, you are awake and in attendance! You are empowered with a newly developed language of emotions, sensations, and thoughts. You can see how important mindful awareness is in your journey to becoming as effective as you can be, especially when dealing with you-know-who.

Jumping ahead, you will learn what can happen when you inform your heightened awareness with an understanding of the narcissist's brain. You'll learn how to confront the narcissist with a knowing-wisdom (empathy) while also keeping him on the hook. In many cases, this is a reasonable approach. But narcissists present themselves along a spectrum. Some are merely annoying, while others are truly perilous and beyond your capacity to influence—in which case mindful awareness may help you see that the relationship is too damaging to sustain. Therefore, chapter 6 looks at dangerous narcissism and how you might need to (safely) disengage from the relationship.

Addressing Perilous and Hypersexual Narcissism: *The Challenges of Shame, Trust, and Betrayal Trauma*

I have spread my dreams under your feet;
Tread softly because you tread on my dreams.

—William Butler Yeats

Under certain circumstances, an intimate relationship with a narcissist isn't worth fighting for, even if you have leverage. At the more severe end of the narcissism spectrum is the narcissist who poses a significant threat to your (and your children's) security, safety, and stability. Perilous and hypersexual narcissists challenge both those in relationship with them and those seeking to treat them. The challenge is even greater when a narcissist is both perilous and hypersexual. This chapter explores how to identify these forms of narcissism, how they affect you, and how to deal with them, including whether you should remain in a relationship with this type of narcissist.

Most often, perilous and hypersexual narcissists are male, not female. Proposed explanations for the disparity include male temperament and greater tendency toward aggression, learned behaviors from primary male role models, social or cultural reinforcement, and biological inclinations in reacting to stress and frustration when schemas are activated.

Perilous and hypersexual narcissists never offer remorse, and in some cases, show no signs of a moral compass. In extreme cases, they may even resemble sociopaths (also known as "antisocial personality disorder"), demonstrating a complete disregard or contempt for others. If you're involved with such a narcissist, please consider making a safety plan to protect yourself and create an avenue for departure from the relationship, even if just a temporary safe place while you sort out what you need to protect yourself (and your children). Be sure to consult confidentially with a legal advocate or attorney who has experience with issues of narcissism.

Identifying Perilous Narcissism

Here is a list of characteristic behaviors of perilous narcissists. Some of the traits include hypersexuality. Read it and carefully consider whether the narcissist in your life engages in these behaviors, and if so, the frequency and extent to which he displays them. If he engages in some less lethal behaviors only occasionally, it might be possible to salvage the relationship. If, however, these behaviors are frequent and pervasive, and particularly if they involve threats to your or another's safety, it's probably best to seek a way out. If you don't know where to turn for help, contact the National Domestic Violence Hotline at 1-800-799-7233.

Threats to Financial and Legal Security

- Gambles excessively

- Spends excessively

- Won't get a job

- Feels entitled to drink and drive

- Buys, uses, or sells illicit drugs

- Views pornography excessively

- Views child pornography

- Has sex with sex workers

- Evades taxes

- Engages in corrupt and fraudulent acts

- Steals

- Engages in pedophilia

Threats to Physical or Emotional Safety

- Engages in physically or verbally abusive behavior

- Threatens to harm you, your children, others, or possibly himself

- Disparages you and your children in public

- Destroys property, throws things, threatens to take the children or leave you penniless; takes out his aggression on pets

- Insists on driving when under the influence of substances, even with you or your children in the car

Threats to Stability in Relationship and the Community

- Has affairs or engages in other promiscuous or risky sexual behavior, including with sex workers, visiting strip clubs, excessive viewing of pornography or cybersex engagement

- Carelessly exposes children to inappropriate material, language, or behaviors

- Lies pathologically about almost anything

- Gets into brawls with neighbors and other community members

- Doesn't display neighborly conduct despite warnings from authorities, for example, playing loud music, having no regard for the distractingly ostentatious or cluttered appearance of his front yard, or being noisy or exhibitionistic

Identifying Hypersexual Narcissism

Many female clients, burdened with sorrow, difficult questions, and fear, come to me with stories about hypersexual narcissism in their lives. They tearfully talk about their partner's sexual transgressions, from infidelity (sometimes with sex workers) to compulsive viewing of pornography (sometimes horrifically aggressive and violent material) to participation in adult chat rooms and frequent visits to strip clubs. Their partners often spend countless hours and thousands of dollars engaging in these sexual behaviors. This behavior is common, and women often feel significant shame about revealing their partner's engagement in it.

Excuses, Excuses

Once discovered, the narcissist typically denies wrongdoing, minimizes the damage, claims all men do it, or blames his partner. Of course, if any of this were true, he could address it in healthier ways—for example, discussing it, seeking help, or even offering the (albeit painful) courtesy of exiting the relationship instead of secretly skulking around. Of course, the narcissist isn't interested in how his partner feels, much less talking about the issue, examining his behavior, or working on it. He avoids imagining the impact of his self-indulgent, disturbing actions on his loved ones, lest he become the "bad guy," which is intolerable. He cannot bear the shame, the responsibility for contributing to your hurt; he cannot ever be "bad" or "wrong"!

So, he asserts that this is just natural male sexuality. Because he is unable to tolerate feeling isolated or emotionally uncomfortable, this is the perfect rationalization. How convenient to be conferred the absolute right to engage in sexual activity beyond his relationship. How convenient to have no control over the demands of his phallic emperor (and how strange that his supreme self-control is held hostage by this one bit of his anatomy). But if his damaging sexual behaviors were just part of being male, then why does he hide them and respond with denial, dismissiveness, defensiveness, and blame when found out?

That said, nature does play a role in holding men's brains hostage on sexual terrain. Writer and philosopher Roger Scruton points out that once people are led by their porn addiction "to see sex in the instrumentalized way that pornography encourages, they begin to lose confidence in their ability to enjoy sex in any other way than through fantasy" (2010, 157).

The brain can be hijacked by sexual stimulation. Data suggests that the addictive and stimulating rush of pleasure from pornography and other sexual activities outside of a partnership can overshadow the pleasure once found in a sexual interlude with one's partner. This feeds the narcissist's chronic need to shut out his deeply rooted loneliness and emptiness—experiences he may see as boredom. When not distracted by other stimuli, he may seek out quick highs, like sex, that eventually may become enduring addictions. But this ravenous desire for stimulation is a distraction from the underlying (and intolerable) emotional hunger that remains unnourished.

No Intimacy Required

The easily accessible world of internet pornography, cybersex chat rooms, and the like, offer plenty of stimuli designed to stroke the male ego, which allows the narcissist to sit atop the pedestal where he feels he belongs. Plus, sexual encounters via pornography, cyber chats, or with sex workers, require no intimacy, giving the narcissist a quick fix with no reciprocity required: there are no expectations, no one he must talk to or interact with authentically, and no one else's needs to consider. Even better, the object of his fantasy will pretend to find him irresistible and act highly aroused by his "sexual prowess" and the size of his bulging...wallet. What a rush for the narcissist—the insatiable approval seeker—to feel extraordinarily desirable.

Drawing the Line

Not all narcissists who engage in hurtful behaviors are perilous-hypersexual narcissists, so it's important to determine where your narcissist lies on the spectrum. When the deceptive activities of a moderate narcissist are discovered, his response is likely to be floundering and fumbling, then angry and blaming, and ultimately dismissive of your concerns. The mighty stud feels justified and entitled to do "simply what all men do."

The perilous-hypersexual narcissist will react similarly, but with more intense anger and volatility, and a lack of shame, remorse, and willingness to change. He may also become aggressive or threatening, engage in increasingly aggressive sexual behavior with you, or show a complete absence of sexual interest.

Deciding Whether to Stay or Go

With a perilous narcissist, safety needs to be your first priority, especially if his volatility, violence, or threats increase; if he is persistent and unremorseful in perpetrating verbal or emotional abuse; or if he responds to your upset contemptuously or hatefully, beyond his chronic disrespect and maltreatment of you.

Many women describe these perilous behaviors as the most heart-breaking and horrifying events in their relationship. Even if they thoughtfully and kindly advocate for peace, the perilous narcissist may only become more callous and menacing. Again, put your safety first and come up with an exit strategy. Many narcissists don the "Prince Charming" mask even in these most difficult times, so it's challenging to assess just how entrenched their perilous behaviors are. The following example provides some insight into how the perilous narcissist twists the truth to absolve himself of highly egregious transgressions.

Samantha and Todd's Story: Hypersexuality and Perilous Narcissism

Samantha and Todd, married for eighteen years, have two young children. After years of kowtowing to her husband's supersized ego, Samantha discovers that Todd has been regularly viewing internet pornography and visiting adult chat rooms. His first response is denial, but Samantha shows him evidence. Todd shifts to defense, shouting, "So what?! All men do it. What's the big deal?" For a change, Samantha doesn't back down. She demands an explanation and says that she won't tolerate this behavior. Perilous narcissism begins to reveal itself as Todd gets enraged. Towering over her, fists clenched, he says, "Trust me, Samantha, you don't want to keep pushing me!"

Samantha maintains her courage and again demands an explanation, and expresses how hurt and betrayed she feels. Unsurprisingly, Todd cruelly places responsibility on Samantha: "Maybe if you weren't such a nag...maybe if you paid more attention to your fat body and cared about our sex life, I wouldn't be looking at porn!"

Crushed, Samantha stares at him incredulously and cries. Todd gets in her face and sneers, "I'm not falling for the tears, Sam. You'd better get a grip! Stop being such a prude and get yourself some serious help. You're nuts! You'll be sorry if you keep pushing me!" Samantha, fighting to feel "felt" by Todd, is awash in anger and pain, so she confronts him again, demanding that he explain himself and promise that he'll stop.

But Todd, remorseless and impervious, declares, "I'm done with this crap and with you!" Kicking a chair and shattering a coffee cup in the sink, he walks out and slams the door.

Samantha drops to the floor, alone, devastated, and sobbing. In the next room, the kids, who have heard everything, sit huddled together and crying.

Eventually Todd returns. A silent and uneasy truce reigns. At first, Samantha's fears of being alone, facing Todd's vengeance if she seeks divorce, and possible joint custody of the children, paralyze her. A nauseated feeling of futility and helplessness twists in her gut. But Samantha has learned something important about Todd, and she uses it to build her resolve. She discreetly seeks legal advice, and with the support of friends, family, and therapy to strengthen her will and confidence, Samantha enters the dreaded legal battle with Todd.

After the divorce, challenges continue. Todd often fails to maintain the visitation schedule because it "interferes with his work," or, more likely, his new party-boy lifestyle. When the kids visit, Todd tells them to do whatever they want, only leave him and his computer alone. Afterward, without bad-mouthing him, Samantha repairs the damage, letting them know that they are entitled to their hurt and confusion, and that their father has problems that he needs to address.

Todd is also predictably late with every alimony and child support payment, so Samantha often has to work overtime. She regrets losing this time with her kids, but she's grateful to have preserved her sanity and safety, and she knows it's important for the kids to have a safe refuge and one healthy parent.

Betrayal Trauma

Usually when we think of trauma, we conjure up images of trauma perpetrated by a stranger, as in a physical or sexual assault, or the trauma associated with certain life events—such as being in a car accident, living in a war zone, or having a health crisis. Trauma can also be experienced vicariously, as in witnessing violence against another. These types of trauma are known as fear-based trauma.

Dr. Jill Manning, one of my go-to experts, defines and differentiates betrayal trauma from fear-based trauma: "Trauma is defined as a deeply distressing or overwhelming experience that is commonly followed by emotional and physical shock. If left unresolved or untreated, traumatic experiences can lead to short- and long-term challenges....[B]etrayal trauma occurs when someone we depend on for survival, or are significantly attached to, violates our trust in a critical way " (Manning 2021).

Betrayal trauma is a violation perpetrated by the very person you would typically turn to for safety, comfort, and protection. It is the person you count on to respect your boundaries, the person you've chosen to live with, to have sex with, and to share your confidences and intimacy with. The violation of trust is personal, whereas in fear-based traumas the violation is committed by a stranger and is often (albeit horrific) a one-time event. With this type of trauma, your *primary other* is often your comforter, your advocate, your ally, and your emotional support as you seek healing.

In betrayal trauma, your primary other perpetrates the event—violates the boundary—and therefore cannot serve as your emotional support. In fact, this person becomes a reminder of the hurtful and devastating reality of the offense he's committed and the broken trust you've experienced. You may also fear recurrent violations, feeling on constant alert for signs of further betrayals. To feel safe, you become chief investigator and steadfast spy—a role you never aspired to, but which feels necessary.

Like fear-based trauma, betrayal trauma can result in some of the same emotional and physiological symptoms:

- Anxiety

- Hypervigilance

- Feeling overwhelmed

- Withdrawal and isolation

- Difficulty concentrating

- Difficulty regulating intense emotions

- Avoidance

- Flashbacks

- Negative thoughts

- Numbness and detachment

- Sleep and appetite disturbances

- Somatic symptoms (e.g., headaches, tremors)

Source: Dr. Jill Manning (2021). https://dr.jillmanning.com/betrayal-trauma/.

Narcissism, Betrayal Trauma, and Intimacy Disorders

Unsurprisingly, narcissistic personality traits are often linked with betrayal trauma, which can include gambling, illicit drug use, a clandestine other life, and hypersexual acting out. These are not just bad habits. Research suggests that these behaviors can escalate to severe addiction when not addressed. Living with someone with compulsive behaviors poses a risk to the stability of a functional relationship. As you just learned, narcissists have a great deal of difficulty with emotional intimacy, stemming from their exiled vulnerability. Let's review how narcissists develop this hyper-sexual mode, as we deepen our understanding of betrayal trauma.

To fully engage in intimate encounters that include an exchange of feelings, exposure to raw truths, eye contact, and expression of terms of endearment, one must have access to personal vulnerability, which brings forth our realness. The narcissist has little to no mastery of personal intimacy and does not easily enter a domain where he cannot reign supreme. Sex becomes a tool for self-soothing and self-distracting, a means of disconnecting from painful emotions, boredom, and stress.

Like many narcissistic behaviors, sex is on his terms only: "I want what I want when I want it." It can be called upon with a keystroke or payment to a sex worker, with no strings attached, no reciprocity, no accountability—and no judgment or measurement for performance.

The rush is experienced through fantasized, fictionalized stories of a very desirable, master-of-the-universe stud—attributes the narcissist seeks as he plants himself in the pixilated image or chat room. Because this soothing and stimulating distraction is so easily accessible—and narcissists tend toward detachment and quick gratification, as well as insufficient self-control, poor boundaries, and a sense of entitlement to do as they please—hypersexual acting out and sex addiction become probable.

Beyond ruptured vows, narcissists who have violated sexual boundaries by secretly viewing pornography or having sexual encounters outside the relationship are likely to deliver calamitous and heartbreaking blows to a partner's self-worth. Partners are forced to make sense out of the person they thought they knew, the one who has violated trust, an essential element in their relationship. Partners may doubt their own worth, and feel shame and self-loathing, as they question why it happened and anticipate other people finding out.

More Than Conflict Management

Betrayal trauma is complicated and often minimized to a "relationship conflict." But it is far more than "No, it's your turn to drive the kids to school," "I always have to empty the dishwasher," or "I am not moving to the suburbs." While these conflicts can cause distress, loneliness, and even heartache, they lack the magnitude of a violation that threatens your emotional safety. Sexual betrayal is probably the most ugly and destabilizing violation for any human to uncover and recover from.

Dr. Manning refers to pornography as "unrighteous dominion." She believes that no human has the right to have their sexuality do harm to another person, because we all have inherent worth. She explains that to use and exploit others for our own personal gain, to objectify them for our own pleasure, requires us to diminish our own humanity, dissociate, and cut ourselves off from reality.

Many sex workers are young women who have been trafficked or abused, or experienced neglect, sexual assault, and/or drug addiction. They are often victims of brutality, rape, disease, and degradation in their roles as sex workers. Additionally, many of the so-called "adult" porn sites host teenaged girls or boys. I share this information with the sexually compulsive narcissistic men I meet in treatment, as part of the psycho-education component for healing. If the hypersexual narcissist is willing to move toward reform, learning these truths and seeing sex workers as victims of subjugation, lifelong abuse, homelessness, addiction, and sex slavery has the capacity to snuff out sexual arousal and to promote remorse and humanity.

Unfortunately, few narcissists, especially the perilous and hypersexual types, opt for reforming their behaviors. This is likely to happen only when the consequences are significant to the narcissist, such as the threat of exposure as a failure, as shameful, or the humiliation of the loss of a loved one, status, or money. In some cases, disciplinary action or legal consequences may lead to mandatory reform, as a result of viewing pornography in the workplace or engaging in child pornography, for example.

Staying with the Narcissist: Reforming the Reformable

If you feel your partner may be capable of change and you choose to stay for now, you don't have to put up with maltreatment. With professional help, the mild/moderate narcissist can heal the wounds of a troubled inner life and learn how to genuinely apologize and change problematic behavior patterns. He can eventually understand the impact of his (hypersexual) behavior on you—the betrayal trauma and how it's affected your feelings toward him and your sexual relationship. But without help, it's unlikely this will ever occur. Rebuilding trust after a breach like this is a threefold endeavor:

1. The offended partner must feel seen, valued, and understood.

2. The offended partner must have a means to rightfully express what she needs to feel safe, to trust again, and to reengage in intimacy.

3. The offended partner will need to (eventually) feel safe enough to acknowledge the narcissist's changes and to recognize and appreciate any efforts made to empathize with her experience and show remorse. We call this "celebrating the victories" to promote enduring positive patterns.

It may seem as if these requirements fall entirely on the shoulders of the betrayed partner. But all three depend on the narcissist's commitment to change and doing the work to make it happen.

For you to feel seen, valued, and understood, you must get a clear sense that your partner knows you from the inside out. He must learn to be empathically attuned. He'll need help—someone to teach him skills to avoid falling into defensiveness and anger, which help him avoid shameful "bad guy" feelings. Without these skills, he will fail.

In order to feel safe to express your needs and embark on the journey of rebuilding trust, the narcissist must find the courage to explore his early experiences. He must look at how he developed his propensity for addictive self-stimulating, and ultimately self-defeating, behaviors. This is necessary to provide, without resentment, the reassurance and transparency necessary for restoring trust. This also puts him in a better position to share with you how he developed this coping mode and what led him down this precipitous path, which will be invaluable in preventing backsliding.

The third requirement—acknowledging the narcissist's changes and appreciating any signs of empathy—may seem the most difficult. Doing this can feel like saying, "Everything's better now. You can go back to being as you were." Remember that you feeling safe is a prerequisite that can only occur if the narcissist makes genuine changes. He must be patient and realize that your reentry into intimacy will be gradual. He must understand that your comfort level will wax and wane, especially when those painful emotions linked to the betrayal are triggered. Finally, he must offer verbal reassurances and continue to acknowledge and accept that he is responsible for the rift between you. In time, you may heal and feel securely reattached to your self-worth, allowing you to be vulnerable with him again. Over time, and with significant work and healing, betrayed partners can begin to integrate reciprocity, generosity, and even forgiveness in the relationship.

Hard to imagine? Indeed, it requires a lot of energy and is not the typical scenario. But, it is possible. I've witnessed this process of transformation as both parties struggle to find their way, making sense out of the conflict, meeting each other's needs, and ultimately creating a relationship that's often better—more real, honest, and satisfying—than it had ever been. The narcissist's internal world is detoxed; the need to be powerful or to hide is evacuated.

Healing isn't fast, and painful feelings surface. Couples engaged in this process often ask how they can deal with this ugly reality that has darkened their relationship. Once they move beyond acute disbelief, anger, and anguish and have agreed on a plan for safety and trust, I ask them to imagine a beautiful architectural structure. I point out that what makes such structures pleasing isn't perfectly laid brick or highly polished stone, but imperfections: bruises in the brick, a medley of colors, or weathered stones. Beautiful structures have stood the test of time and been cared for by people who cherish them. This is an apt metaphor for an enduring relationship: sturdy despite the challenges to its foundation, rich with colors of both brilliance and sorrow, with imperfections that express a raw honesty, and, most of all, painstakingly cared for by those who want it to last.

If you have children, your love and concern for them can be a tremendous motivator for working hard to mend the damage narcissism has wrought in your relationship. Unfortunately, desperate to feel safe, children often assume the position of marital arbiters. Be careful not to allow them to function in this way. As you've learned, the effects of narcissistic anger, entitlement, and disparagement on children can be quite damaging. Many children mimic a narcissistic parent and internalize that parent's style of thinking and interacting. Alternatively, children may take on problematic traits and coping styles of a parent who is passive, self-sacrificing, or fails to provide protection.

Leaving the Narcissist

If you have opted to leave the narcissist in your life or are about to, you know it can be truly terrifying. Divorce can be contentious, but divorcing a narcissist is even more daunting and dramatic because the narcissist usually makes the process as arduous and anguished as possible—even though parting with money is as difficult, if not more so, as parting with you. This embittered process is especially problematic when *you* end the relationship. The divorce process is chock-full of conflict, which allows the narcissist to stay connected and competitive. You become the consummate opponent, and to this not-so-soon-to-be ex, it is all about winning the game. Remember, for the narcissist, any perception or experience of losing, failure, rejection, being controlled, or being left alone is worthy of counterattack and punishment. Sadly, many of the narcissistic men I have treated came to recognize that their partner is/was one of the most caring, needs-meeting, supportive, and healthy matches they could have chosen—and yet their narcissism squandered it all.

Myth Buster: Narcissists Will Leave You

Narcissists do not typically end relationships, despite countless threats to do so. They end relationships only when (1) they already have someone waiting in the wings, or (2) they have enough fans and followers to fill the gap. Most just fill the air with their insolent bluster to keep you fearful and acquiescent.

Many of my (offended) clients report that they fear ending the relationship or seeking professional help because they predict the narcissist will just launch into a tirade, pack his bags, leave, and then punish them. And, yes, many narcissists will launch into anger and may even threaten to leave when they sense a power play, but few will actually leave except under the conditions I just mentioned. If the tirade is not dangerous to your safety, you might insist on professional help to aid the process. The sturdier and calmer your demeanor, the more serious your message becomes. The narcissist cannot just walk away or blame it on "your massive paranoia and insecurity about what I'm looking at on my devices," "your neediness," or "your super sensitivity to everything I say."

No, this time he will hear you, and he will need to carefully measure the weight of what he is up against. He needs to hear that you are *really* done; it's over.

Professional Help

Narcissists usually only agree to seek the help of a professional because they believe this will satisfy your "itch" and get things back to status quo. The mediator or therapist must have experience dealing with narcissism so they can bring the reality of relationship termination into the room, manage the reactions, maintain the leverage, and navigate the turbulent waters going forward.

A mediator, therapist, or attorney who is experienced with narcissism knows that the narcissist must ultimately feel that *they* (the narcissist) made this decision or that the decision is mutual. Experts know that the narcissist must be spared feeling like the "loser" or the "bad guy" by proposing all agreements as being something the narcissist already knows: "You must have already thought of this, Joe. You're a bright guy and you know what it takes. I know you want to do the right thing to protect your family—and, of course, you both deserve to be happy."

Some of you may see this as fueling the narcissism, or what I often refer to as the "when all else fails, get your vomit bucket ready" technique. It may make you queasy to imagine such words being imparted to the one who has caused so much hurt and devastation. But if you want the narcissist to get out of his own way and do the right thing by you (and your children), he is not likely to come to these fair and reasonable conclusions on his own. He will remain fiercely affixed to a retaliation mission without a counterintuitive appeal to his wounded ego.

There is no guarantee that these strategies will work with all narcissists, but they work for many, and they are certainly worth a try. In my work, I have met too many betrayed partners who have either suffered the harrowed proceedings of a two- to ten-year divorce (some with, and most without, satisfying results), or who forfeited their rights or simply surrendered in exchange for emotional peace and forward motion. Perhaps you know the hardships suffered—including shared custody with someone reckless, who carelessly allows his children to be exposed to inappropriate material, who uses them as vengeance pawns and attempts to alienate them from you—all of this in the lingering aftermath of the "how dare you make me the bad guy" condemnation.

Many professionals will recommend that, in preparation for divorcing a narcissist, you consider doing the following:

- **Put safety first.** If you are in an abusive or dangerous relationship, consider getting a protective restraining order from the courts.

- **Document.** Keep emails, text messages, video clips, and any other important documentation of infidelity, addiction, gambling, spending, illicit drug use, physical or emotional abuse, or any misappropriations of personal and financial agreements. Consider having copies secured, perhaps outside of the home, of all checking and savings account statements, tax returns, insurance policies, credit card statements, deeds and titles, and your passport and birth certificate.

- **Protect passwords.** Change the passwords on your phone, laptop, other devices, social media, and email. Limit your exposure on social media, as much as possible. Your privacy will be critical to having the support you need without worrying that the narcissist is collecting and twisting evidence to use against you.

- **Plan ahead.** Open a new bank account and design a future budget so that you may be thoughtful in your expectations and proposals regarding financial settlements. Consider the financial, social, and emotional costs versus benefits of staying in your current home or moving to a new residence.

- **Seek co-parenting support.** Identify family and child therapists, parenting experts, self-help organizations, support groups, peer groups, and online communities that offer specific assistance for co-parenting with a narcissistic partner. Chapter 8 will address the challenges of co-parenting with a narcissist (whether living together or apart).

- **Consult with appropriate experts.** Seek out a mediator, attorney, or therapist/legal advocate who specializes in divorcing a narcissist. If you seek your own private attorney, arrange for an initial consultation so that you can answer these questions:

  - What is their experience dealing with issues of narcissism, and can they provide examples?

  - What is their accessibility—do they actually quarterback your case and respond to your calls, or do they delegate everything to a junior associate?

  - What can you expect in terms of cost, time, and unique strategies they use to manage narcissistic manipulations and get a reasonable outcome?

- Are they able to recommend specialists who are also sensitive to narcissism, should there be any orders for child-custody-visitation evaluations?

- What is their position on contact versus no contact when divorcing a narcissist? (Your lawyer should carefully assess when it might be beneficial to have contact with the narcissist in order to employ the "when all else fails" strategies—the ones, albeit nauseating, that appeal to the narcissist's ego without selling your soul.)

Whether a lawyer or divorce mediator assists you, your advocate should be fluent in issues of narcissism because the narcissist is often fluent in charm, swagger, solicitation, spinning webs (gaslighting), and word crafting. You need someone who is trained to see through the glossy finish and who can confront intimidating and threatening verbiage—basically someone who does not get captivated by the narcissist nor side-swiped by their game.

While divorce mediation can be cost-saving, efficient, and grounded in the notion of fairness, cooperation, and creative compromise, it is, unfortunately, a problematic option when divorcing a narcissist. Being rejected escalates "you'll be sorry" threats, while fighting against the feeling of shame activates both the "I'm not the bad guy" and "you gave me no choice" refrains. Nonetheless, mediation is always worth a try, given all the benefits, especially if you can locate a divorce mediator who is well-versed in dealing with narcissistic clients. However, be prepared to move on to a savvy specialist attorney if mediation fails.

Conclusion

If you're in a relationship with a hypersexual or perilous narcissist, I cannot overemphasize the importance of caring for your safety and that of your children, if you have them. That said, the narcissist's charm and gaslighting can make it difficult to determine whether he is truly unredeemable. Observe him closely and mindfully—in the moment and not through the filters of your past. If you think you might get through to him and he may be capable of change, use the communication skills in this book to engage the wounded, damaged person within, and use your leverage to get him to seek professional help.

If you elect to stay and try to salvage the relationship, empathy (not sympathy) will be one of your most effective tools in fostering change. Chapter 7 outlines a strategy for utilizing empathy while ensuring that your own needs are met and appropriate limits are set.

Should you choose to leave, prepare yourself with thoughtful exit strategies offered in this chapter. Finding a legal advocate with a proficiency in narcissism will not be easy, so carefully scrutinize your options. But it is refreshing to see how many lawyers do list themselves on the internet as "experts in dealing with narcissism." Lawyers can also consult with narcissism experts who can assist in scripting effective psychological and emotional language to integrate with legalese.

Co-parenting with a narcissist can be another emotional hurdle, one that finds us weighty in exasperation and lean in expertise. Chapter 8 looks at common challenges when co-parenting with a narcissist, and offers effective strategies, whether living together or apart.

CHAPTER 7

Using Empathic Confrontation: *A Winning Strategy for Interpersonal Effectiveness*

If we could read the secret history of our enemies, we should find in each man's life sorrow and suffering enough to disarm all hostility.

—Henry Wadsworth Longfellow

E ven if the narcissist in your life doesn't fall into the perilous category, in his less-than-charming Mr. Hyde mode, it can feel like being with an enemy. Schemas get triggered, leaving you woozy, speechless, or at the end of your rope. Narcissists can suck the oxygen right out of the room. Being angry and fed up temporarily thickens your skin, but carrying anger around can become exhausting. Before you know it, the fatigue brings you right back to feeling raw and powerless. So, you surrender and wait for him to (hopefully) return to the honeymooning mode where he is charming and present.

However, with your new mindfulness and communication skills, you have options. You can remain unwavering in the storm—refusing to compromise your values or integrity. The bottom line is that you have rights, valid needs and desires, and inherent value. You matter, and you're worth sticking up for!

But to be effective and achieve rewarding outcomes, you need more than a fit mind and attuned inner wisdom; you need to "get" who the narcissist is. You need more than an intellectual understanding; you need an emotional literacy about his inner world and experience. It's like feeling his mind inside of yours (something you may not want to do with a perilous narcissist). This isn't mind reading; this is emotional wisdom or empathy.

Before you read on, one important note: This approach is inappropriate with anyone who makes you feel unsafe or abused. That calls for a completely different protocol, often requiring exit strategies and safety plans. If the narcissist in your life is violent, abusive, or threatens your safety in any way, please seek assistance immediately. If you don't know where to turn for help, contact the National Domestic Violence Hotline at 1-800-799-7233.

Distinguishing Between Empathy and Compassion

There is considerable confusion around the term "empathy." Many people use it interchangeably with "compassion." Both words may involve bearing witness to another person's suffering or joy, but the two are quite different in ways that are highly pertinent to any discussion of narcissism.

Many clients are taken aback when I advocate using empathy with narcissists. They mistakenly think I'm asking them to feel sorry for the bully who tortured them. So, let's take a moment to differentiate empathy from compassion.

Empathy is to truly *understand* the experience of another. It doesn't mean that you necessarily agree with, condone, or support the other person's feelings and behavior, simply that you understand them in a "felt" way. In an empathic state, you have knowledge. You experience the thoughts, feelings, and sensations of another. It's as if you can feel the person's experience resonating within yourself. You are fully attuned.

Let's say a dear friend and colleague arrives at work visibly upset. She describes a car accident she almost had while driving to work. She can visualize the truck coming toward her and the split second in which she evaded it by steering into the shoulder. She describes how she stopped to help a less-lucky motorist who was struck badly. She cries as she talks about the what-ifs and how lucky she feels to be alive and safe. Nervously laughing, she says, "Imagine, being so happy to be here at work on a Monday morning." You tell her you're happy she's okay and that you can only imagine how terrifying it must have been.

You picture the scenario as she describes it, along with all of the what-ifs. You feel your body clenching as she describes the sound of horns blaring and the impact of the truck crashing into the other car just a few feet away. Your heart rate elevates at the thought of a phone call reporting that your friend had been badly injured or killed. You might even recall a similar event in your own life. You know the pain she endured as a teen when she lost a sibling to a tragic motorcycle accident, and how hard she'd worked to deal with her unimaginable grief and the grief of her parents. She says she'll be okay after a moment to catch her breath and grab some coffee, but you can feel her desire to seek calm and relief; it rises within you too. You get it. This is empathy—this is emotional, sensorial wisdom.

Compassion goes further. It's a radiating desire to console, comfort, and alleviate the pain and suffering of another. It's rooted in empathic sensing where you have a clear felt sense of the other person's experience, followed by sympathy (defined as sorrow in response to your empathic sensing) for the other person's misfortune. Compassion is the tendency to move beyond empathy; it means feeling compelled to extend a kindness, do something about the person's pain, or bring relief.

In the previous example, with compassion you would comfort your friend, offer a hug, and say, "Please, let me get you coffee. Why don't you just sit down and take a few quiet moments for yourself? I'll cover for you. And let me know if there's anything else I can do, even if you just need to talk." With compassion, it's difficult to walk away without desiring, imagining, or executing some plan or action for relief.

It can be daunting to employ empathy and compassion in your relationship with a narcissist, given how rarely narcissists expose their vulnerability. Yet the ability to experience empathy (and even perhaps compassion when vulnerability is exposed) for this troubling and troubled person is just the skill you need to achieve more satisfying interactions—and hopefully a more satisfying relationship.

Feeling "Felt"

A child's healthy development is contingent upon a parent or caregiver providing an attuned emotional connection—in other words, empathy. As a child looks into her parent's eyes for comfort or approval, the parent consciously reflects an understanding of her experience. The parent accepts and validates the child's feelings or needs and helps her make sense of what's happening within her: "Of course, sweetie, I know it's very scary to see monsters on your bedroom wall, and you don't want to be alone with them. Let's go and see if maybe it's just those silly shadows dancing in the moonlight again."

When the child's need for attuned connection isn't adequately met, she feels misunderstood, invisible, worthless, lonely, or ashamed of longing for connection, which can lead to painful self-labels, such as "weak," "foolish," or "unlovable," and self-defeating life patterns, such as detachment, avoidance, or bullying. Feeling that others get you is crucial for the cultivation of empathic awareness, which is essential for healthy emotional and interpersonal development.

A key aspect of narcissism is seeking visibility, but in a maladaptive way. In the absence of feeling understood, or "gotten," narcissists search for approval, primarily from their performance. They fight for special entitlements as proof of their success and extraordinariness. They seek absolute control and emotional autonomy, deriving a sense of power from not needing anyone. There is a deep well of shame attached to their quashed but very human longing to be understood, visible, loved, and accepted. Their unmet need for attuned emotional connection and their undeveloped understanding of their own emotional autobiography leaves them without empathy.

Rather than tuning in to others, the narcissist remains caught up in the pursuit of approval: *How am I doing? She really likes me. I impressed him—really nailed it. I wonder if they like what I just said. Uh-oh, I think I'm in trouble. I'll show them.* This "all about me" focus prevents the narcissist from truly engaging in interactions, much less experiencing or conveying empathy. As a result, those around him feel unseen, lonely, empty, and frustrated.

Almost all humans possess the capacity for empathy. Fostering empathy in a narcissist isn't impossible, but it's challenging. It requires an expert who understands narcissism and is competent in working with this population. Unfortunately, getting narcissists to agree to go to therapy is usually difficult. It takes strong leverage—meaningful consequences, such as losing someone or something important, and enforcing those consequences if they don't get help.

Again, empathy doesn't mean agreeing with or condoning their actions; it simply requires understanding. To this end, we mentally and emotionally conjure up an image, story, or bodily sensation that allows us to imagine the experiences or intentions of others. We become emotionally, mentally, and physically engaged in making sense out of what we see and hear, whether it's a character in a movie, a loved one, or perhaps even the person in the mirror. This lights a path to meaning and unburdens us of misappropriated responsibility, blame, toxic anger, shame, helplessness, and guilt. We must have access to our vulnerable side to take in the pain or joy of another. This is often an impasse for the narcissist.

Empathy creates clarity and awareness of what is real, freeing us from the distorted perceptions imposed by our schemas. This opens the door to emotional relief and clears the path toward personal transformation.

This state of "knowing," of emotional and mental sensibility, provides much-needed balance when dealing with a narcissist. His behavior has the power to bring up old, schema-driven beliefs and feelings that make you doubt who you are, your worth, and perhaps even your capacity to be in a relationship. You may fear expressing your opinions or feel ashamed if your ideas aren't as "bold" or "clever" as his. Because empathy allows you to deeply understand the narcissist, it's the perfect antidote, fortifying you to stand your ground, hold him accountable, and not take responsibility for his issues. Best of all, you can interact with him without the burden of exhausting anger, defensiveness, or submissiveness. You get him. You may feel badly for him and might even tell him that, but without giving in or giving up your rights.

With time, your empathy—your felt sense of the narcissist's suffering—may even deepen, moving you toward compassion. This doesn't always happen—it depends on how your heart has weathered the harsh storms of narcissism. If the damage is reparable, you may find yourself wanting to help, comfort, accept, or even forgive. Sometimes this is perfectly appropriate; it might even be necessary, as long as it doesn't violate your nonnegotiable rights and values.

A Brief Look at the Science of Empathy

In the 1980s and 1990s, neuroscientists discovered an intriguing type of neuron that is activated both when we perform a certain action, such as grasping a cup or smiling, and when we observe someone else performing the same action (Iacoboni 2009). It's as if the brain is responding to our own reflection in a mirror, so these cells are called mirror neurons.

Recent studies on empathy utilizing functional magnetic resonance imaging scans suggest that context and individual makeup, including biology, personality traits, and emotional states, play a role in the degree to which an individual can access empathic awareness. Apparently, connecting and attuned responses (prosocial responses) are sometimes overshadowed by the motivation to seek revenge or punish, especially when perceptions of unfairness or intentional harm are present.

What does this tell us about the narcissist? Perhaps his need to protect himself keeps him walled off from painfully disturbing emotions, especially those that make him feel that he isn't meeting your needs. When you tearfully express your pain, his annoyance, schemas, and locked-down emotional state keep him virtually blindfolded. As portrayed in the following case example, the narcissist may be unable to tolerate seeing or sensing your feelings; he dodges his own vulnerability, and instantaneously flips into a self-righteous mode of angry sighs and dismissive retorts. You may even be on the receiving end of a retaliation that arises from his sense that you're intentionally trying to make him feel bad about himself.

Sue and Don's Story

Don has just learned from his stepsister that his father is dying. His lifelong distressful relationship with that demanding, never-satisfied man who never once told him he loved him is coming to an end. Don's wife, Sue, watches as Don harrumphs into the phone, rolling his eyes as his stepsister expresses sadness and sympathy.

For years, Sue has observed Don's coldness whenever anyone, herself included, shared a caring or concerned emotion with him. She used to feel annoyed and sometimes hurt by Don's coldness, but she's come to realize that it's Don's issue, not hers, and that in this moment he is trying not to feel the intolerable pain of letting go of the fantasy that his father might someday tell Don that he always loved him and was proud of him. Sue knows that Don won't be able to acknowledge this fantasy or accept the loss without professional help; he finds it too shameful to admit that he needs his dad—or anyone, for that matter.

Sue sees the look on his face, hears his dismissive grunt, and recognizes a familiar pattern. She can also empathically relate his feelings to her own childhood, recalling that her dad would often get home late at night extremely drunk. She recalls how he would storm into her room, waking her and yelling at her for some minor or imagined infraction. Her mother, in the neighboring bedroom, silently waited her turn to be admonished. With no one to protect her, Sue had to be strong as she heard her dad yelling and throwing things in the next room. Once the chaos died down, Sue's older sister would tiptoe into her room and remind her that she just needed to be quiet and be a good girl. She told her not to worry, "The sun will come out tomorrow." Sue remembers her own inner harrumphing when her sister left the room: Who cares? Nothing will ever change! No, no, wait. I'll try harder. I will. I promise.

Even though her experience was quite different from Don's, it created a resonance that allowed Sue to understand his desire to avoid any unearthing of the fear and hurt buried within. His tone, posture, gestures, and facial expression offered a sensory understanding of his stoic entrapment. And although she felt a desire to comfort Don, she knew that he would resist. She no longer would take that personally. She had done a lot of work and had come to realize that emotional release wasn't a sign of being foolish, overly sentimental, or ignorant, as Don had so often said when she expressed her feelings, fears, and vulnerability.

Sue had also succeeded in getting Don to quit making derogatory statements. With courage, patience, and empathy, she had helped him see the origins of his behavior—years of living with a demanding and depriving dad, and a yielding mom. She had disconnected from interactions anytime Don hurled demeaning labels. Still, he continued to flamboyantly express his discomfort in nonverbal terms. Because Sue now understood that this wasn't about her and could link Don's emotions to her own painful early experiences, she actually found his expressions useful, as they revealed, in a felt way, that Don was struggling. As always, Don attempted to hide his struggle. Because he refused any self-examination or therapy, he remained a prisoner of his memories and an obedient servant to his coping method of being tough and independent and dutifully attempting to conceal all upsetting emotions.

Yet Don's desire to stuff his emotions was like trying to silence a toddler who wants your attention when you're on the phone. Tugging and crying, the child wails unrelentingly until you notice. As a parent, you have some options: You could attempt to force silence with intimidation or threats, although the result may be a withered state of surrender. Alternatively, you might gather the child on your lap to soothe him while you continue your conversation. Or, if he's in great distress, you might hang up and lovingly attend to him.

Don, who was on the receiving end of the first type of parenting response, learned early on how to stuff his feelings and self-soothe with distractions. Now, as an adult, he engages in a variety of self-soothing behaviors, like drinking too much, spending countless hours online, and buying technical gadgets, all to silence his "nagging" emotions and stuff them into submission.

Sue has a keen empathy for Don's reactions and responses, even though she doesn't like them and doesn't find them helpful to their relationship. In fact, these behaviors are damaging their sex life. Because Don lacks empathy, not just for Sue, but also for himself, his destructive and detached coping habits remain entrenched. His walls make Sue feel more and more shut out, and she finds it difficult to be drawn to him when he offers a playful invitation for a sexual interlude. Of course, Don feels shut out when Sue rejects his advances, so he rolls his eyes, grunts, and turns away, perpetuating and deepening the

pattern. This situation can't be resolved until Don develops some
empathy for Sue and the loneliness she feels. His lack of awareness
isn't for lack of effort on Sue's part. Countless times she's tried to tell
Don that she feels locked out and alone and simply can't switch into
an excited sexual mode in the absence of emotional intimacy. She
needs to know him and sense that he knows her. She understands this
is difficult with someone who has issues of narcissism.

Mirroring the Other

Shared human experiences are opportunities for wisdom, which provides
a gateway to freedom from false beliefs, distractions, and self-defeating
behaviors. Once our mental vision is clear, we can see the strengths and
struggles others experience. When this clarity and empathy emerge in a
relationship, people become mirrors for one another. We all thrive on
seeing ourselves accurately reflected and held in the mind and heart of
another. We all want to feel understood—not judged, ignored, or belit-
tled—for who we are and how we experience and respond to the world,
even if it may seem silly sometimes. This is what builds a foundation that
can withstand the weighty and painful triggers we face in our most important relationships.

Consider what might happen if Don makes a sexual advance and Sue
responds, "I'm sorry, but I'm not interested right now. I know it upsets you,
but it's difficult for me to feel aroused when I've felt so alone for so long.
When you stay locked away in your own world, I feel completely shut out.
I wish I felt more included. When I don't know how you're feeling or what
you're thinking, it gets really lonely for me."

Don will likely hear this through his defectiveness filter as *You're an*
asshole who only thinks of yourself, and you're a failure as a partner. But what
if instead he could empathically sense Sue's struggle and bypass the feelings of inadequacy and helplessness? That might garner a different
response: "Sue, I get it. When I'm cut off and distant, it makes you feel
very alone, and that makes it hard to feel close to me sexually. I know that

it's really important to you that I share more of my feelings and show more interest in you. I know that we deal with being upset very differently, and it doesn't work well for you, or for us, when I shut down. I may not always get it, but I can sense that struggle in you. I know how much pain you've already endured with your dad, who was supposed to be there for you."

I know you're probably thinking, *Yeah, right...the narcissist in my life would never respond that way.* The fact is, you're probably right; it's extremely unlikely without professional help or meaningful leverage. Unfortunately, even with professional help, this kind of transformation may be impossible. All too often, narcissists' relationships end up encrusted in an eroded, decaying framework that simply cannot be repaired.

The Narrator Voice

If hope still abides and the narcissist commits to therapy or self-examination, you may wonder how to express your appreciation while maintaining sufficient leverage so he won't assume everything is better and drop out of treatment prematurely. The solution is to celebrate the little victories of budding awareness and change in a direct, balanced way.

The narrator in a play is the one who sets the stage, targeting our attention to appreciate what is about to happen. When rebuilding trust with a narcissist, your "narrator voice" can also set the stage by crafting language that expresses your intentions. This language conveys both what you *don't* intend for the narcissist to experience—such as overzealous optimism, criticism, or control—as well as what you *do* intend for him to understand—such as your slowly emerging hope, cautious optimism, and healing process.

Perhaps by saying something like, "I can see that you're making an effort to be more considerate of my feelings and opinions. I appreciate that, and it makes me feel closer to you. But I'm not sure how to share this without making it sound like everything is okay. I don't want to ignore what you're doing, but I also don't want to give the impression that everything is fine. I need to know that you can understand my dilemma."

Beautiful use of the "narrator voice"! Your narrator delivers the message, the struggle, the mixed feelings living inside of you. The narrator thinks (carefully) out loud. The narrator does not react.

The narrator can also establish leverage as you describe (out loud) the wish to have a satisfying and lasting relationship—"I would love for us to grow old together, lovingly and happily"—and the sadness you feel knowing you will inevitably separate if healing work is not employed.

Under His Skin: Experiencing the Narcissist's Inner World

Brace yourself! Here comes the *real* challenge. I often tell clients about the sense of unfairness they may experience, in the early phases of treatment, by bearing so much of the burden to cultivate an experiment for change. I say, "You must light the torch and lead the way for transformation to occur," meaning they must tediously work at maintaining leverage, crafting empathic language for effective confrontation and limit setting. However, they shouldn't have to carry that torch forever—the narcissist must reciprocate and become receptive. Throughout the process, you must carefully evaluate progress and decide whether it's meeting your needs. You always have the right to change your mind and decide enough is enough. Start your day with a few deep breaths, a sturdy posture, and a conscious awareness of whatever you are choosing for that day. Tomorrow, you may choose differently, or not.

I know—it's a tall order. But if the narcissist plays a significant role in your life, it may feel important to know you've done all that you could before calling it quits. And now that you've chosen to peruse the biography aisle of your emotional library rather than the (schema-laden) fiction aisle, you can better appreciate the strengths and struggles of both the narcissist and yourself, and remain grounded in truth.

Empathically understanding the narcissist does not mean excusing obnoxious behaviors. It means trying to genuinely feel his inner world in order to escape the trap of personalizing these actions as your fault. Specific techniques can help. For example, when the narcissist addresses you sharply, you could superimpose the face of an unloved little boy over that of the grown man before you. As you picture the child's face, try to imagine his pain, his sense of defectiveness and shame, his loneliness and emotional emptiness, and the impossible standards he had to meet for attention, love, or approval confusingly mixed with the message that he is perfect. You summon your empathy and embrace the vulnerability that the man before you cannot bear to consciously feel. In so doing, you are clear about the motivational drivers and schema triggers likely responsible for his actions, or lack thereof. You can point toward that understanding with phrases like, "I know you're uncomfortable, but it's not okay for you to be dismissive." Another quick empathic response might be, "I can see this is very important to you, and I'd like to hear more about it, but I cannot do that when you are expressing it so angrily or by attacking me. That's not acceptable."

This brilliant strategy is utilized in treatment by a therapist. The therapy relationship serves as a microcosm of the world outside. Behaviors such as resistance, showing off, detaching, bullying, criticalness, and entitlement are all addressed by a schema therapist who is postured as a *limited reparenting* agent—"seeing the child within." This strategy was a gift from Dr. Jeffrey Young. When reparenting the narcissist, emphasis is placed upon nurturing the lonely and deprived child hidden within, doing so with both caring and guidance. Limited reparenting includes empathy and setting limits, experiences the narcissist didn't have as a child, modeling ways he can nurture and care for this part of himself. This heals damaging schemas and reorganizes the way the child is cradled or exiled in memory. Building on this strategy, I begin to request childhood photos that we could utilize in treatment. Seeing the real child, alongside their personal narrative, enables me to maintain my *good parent* mode, which affords me the stamina to effectively engage, confront, discipline, model, and set limits without my personal activations getting in the way.

Summoning empathy (and possibly even compassion) is an extremely helpful tool for maintaining an even keel when he starts to tip the boat. Try to hold an image of the vulnerable child in your mind while the adult before you is once again carelessly sputtering about something. You'll know that what typically drives his drama is a need to avoid the feelings of that little guy behind the scenes—his own vulnerability, which he regards as pathetic and inadequate, and his intolerance for frustration and discomfort. You can feel that the child is frightened, sad, ashamed, and deprived, perhaps spoiled too. While doing this, you remain poised in your competent, worthy, and healthy adult mode. You can better express your rights, your needs, and draw a line in the sand if need be. The transformation is slow, but over time as you continue to abort the dance and drop new seeds in the soil, you may begin to witness a new bend and flex. Moreover, you'll see yourself with affirmed and healthy righteousness, no longer drowning in self-doubt or exhausted by your high-octane anger that, when expressed virulently, only fuels the narcissist's love of the game.

In William Wordsworth's lyrical poem "My Heart Leaps Up," he says, "The Child is father of the Man" (1892, 200). Perhaps he was talking about the inner child presiding over the mind of the grown man, just like a schema or an outdated template for living. Without a discerning awareness, the adult narcissist takes his cues from the child within—allowing painful early experiences to haunt his relationships in the present.

Here's a tip: Try the photograph strategy for yourself. Obtain a photo of the narcissist as a child. This can be very useful in strengthening your empathic knowledge base and your emotional wellness. It's also good to have a photo of yourself as a child to remind you that the vulnerable part within you also needs your empathy, compassion, and care. You can have a peek at little you each day, but tuck her or him safely away when confronting the narcissist—imagine a safety bubble or other secure place where the vulnerable you will not have to bear responsibility for challenging grown-up interactions. Some even laminate their pictures and keep them as handy visual cues during this phase of healing, growth, and change.

Keeping the Narcissist on the Hook

Utilizing empathy doesn't mean letting the narcissist off the hook when he's behaving badly. Understanding and emotional generosity are necessary, but it's equally important to hold the narcissist accountable. Essentially, you want to aim for confrontation from an empathic stance. The following five vignettes will illustrate how to use empathic confrontation with the narcissist in your life. Feel free to recast the narcissist to be relevant to your situation. Each scenario focuses on a different skill for achieving more satisfying and authentic outcomes:

- Differentiating between fault and responsibility

- Setting limits

- Establishing the rules of reciprocity

- Promoting optimal awareness by providing positive feedback

- Integrating an essential element: the raw truth

Differentiating Between Fault and Responsibility

Your husband, Steven, arrives twenty minutes late to pick you up at the train station. Without offering a greeting, explanation, or apology, he yells at you about how he's never going to do this again: "I swear, Sharon, don't even start with me. I had to leave my associates at the country club, forgot my cell phone, waded through obnoxious traffic, and now I'm dealing with the your sour attitude. Who needs this!"

You smack him in the head with your purse, jump out of the car, and get back on the train, never to see him again. Okay, with the fantasy out of your system...let's move on to a more productive strategy.

You give Steven a chance to hear the echo of his ugliness against the silence, while you gather your composure. You remind yourself that this isn't about you. Steven has stepped in his own way again. You glance over at him just long enough to catch a glimpse of the lost little boy underneath his mean and scowling veneer. You take an easy breath, engage your empathy, and say, "I understand how important it is for you to protect yourself from embarrassment with your associates, and from the dread of letting me down. True, I was annoyed—and a bit worried too. I'm sure it was frustrating to not have your phone to call me. I understand that you expect me to be angry because you're late. Steven, I care about your feelings, even the aggravation of dealing with traffic. But it's difficult for me to feel any tenderness for you when you're so hostile. I'd like to feel connected, but to do that I need you to communicate with more consideration for my feelings as well as your own. Once you've had a chance to calm down, I'd appreciate an apology, and then we can brainstorm how to manage this issue in the future."

The momentary silence appears to be seeding some thoughts. Do you perhaps detect a brief sobered look on his face before he says, "Oh please, don't hit me with that psychobabble stuff about my feelings again. I'm angry because I knew this would happen, and I also knew that you'd be pissed off if I didn't pick you up. That's all. Don't make it my fault. I had a lot on my plate today too."

Maybe you're back to that fantasy, where you smack him upside the head. I know—this is hard work. Nevertheless, you again patiently assign him responsibility without faulting him: "Look, Steven, I appreciate that you agreed to help me out today. I'm not blaming you for what you couldn't control or for feeling upset. However, it is your responsibility to figure out how to express those feelings without blaming me or putting me down. Doing otherwise is simply unacceptable. This behavior is hurtful to me and to our marriage."

He is quiet again, then nods slowly. A break in the storm? He drives on and mutters a soft, "Yeah, okay."

Well…it's a beginning.

In this scene, you had the schema-proof shelter of your steady and wisely discerning mind. You have mastered the trigger that would have made you feel helpless and angry. You sense certain schema-driven reflexes in your fantasy response, but your understanding of Steven's issues, your love for him, and your compassionate advocacy for yourself have enabled you to rescript this interaction. You emphasize responsibility over fault, and you call attention to the validity of your own needs. You also offer understanding and generosity to the shamed little boy who wants to be liked and appreciated. After all, you've chosen to work on saving your marriage at this point in time.

Again, this is very hard work. Though you can probably identify with scenarios like this one, you may predict a less favorable outcome or feel dissatisfied with the way it concluded. And while it's not enough yet, it's a start. Habits are tough to change—for you both. The brain is a malleable organ, but it takes time, repetition, and effort to create enduring changes. For change to occur, you need to look at how long you've been driving in the same gear, unable to mount the steep incline. Sometimes you have to switch gears to gain momentum. New ways of communicating may feel contrived at first, but they can become your signature lyrics over time if they reflect your wise and affirmed voice. One client described the power of being present in a calm and centered mind as feeling like "waking up alive," meaning he could feel what was happening in the moment rather than feel deadened by his old, maladaptive tapes.

Setting Limits

When your daughter is just an infant, your boss calls and needs you to travel out of town on business. This is the first time you'll be away from your daughter overnight, and you're wracked with guilt and worry. Because your husband works nights and you didn't have enough notice to line up a caregiver, you reluctantly agree to let your mother-in-law care for the baby. But when you call home to check in, you're confronted with a tyranny of shoulds, musts, and have-tos from your mother-in-law. If it wasn't so insulting, it might be humorous that your mother-in-law actually moved the dresser and nightstand out of the baby's room because they lacked a good feng shui vibe.

It's painful, but the incident motivates you to learn how to set limits using empathic confrontation. You begin by trying to understand her behavior and its roots in her past. Then you hold her accountable for her actions in the present. When you return home, you tell her how much you appreciate her help. Then you address her troublesome behavior: "I also appreciate how important it is for you to maintain certain standards, and I admire what you've done in your home. However, we'd appreciate it if you wouldn't impose your standards on our home. I'm happy that you and the baby are forming a relationship, but please respect our parenting and household decisions, even if you don't agree with them. If you aren't sure about something, feel free to ask us. This will help us protect our relationship and not carry any resentments."

You may be thinking, *Are you kidding me? The narcissist in my life would just ignore me, tell me off, or start World War III if I said something like that.* Yet even if she does respond in these ways, you can continue to set limits while responding with whatever empathy you can muster. If the narcissist ignores you or is condescending, you can say something like, "I know you aren't used to having people challenge you, and I'm not looking to have a debate. I'm just respectfully letting you know that this subject isn't open to negotiation. I'm sorry if that upsets you. That isn't my intention." If she resorts to anger or aggression, establish that you won't tolerate threatening treatment. Maintaining your calm, simply say, "This conversation can't continue if you speak to me that way." If she persists, hang up or walk away. At least you'll know that you tried to improve the relationship. Of course, if the narcissist is your in-law, you'll also need the cooperation of your partner. You will need to present a united front in any attempts to set limits. Remember, leverage is critical when the narcissistic stance seems impenetrable. What can you take away that will have meaning to them, if they cannot respect your needs and rights? Perhaps limited access to the grandchildren, to you, and/or to your partner.

Establishing the Rules of Reciprocity

It's Saturday night and your boyfriend, Chris, announces that you'll both be dining at his favorite restaurant—again. You have, for the most part, been a good sport about this. You know how critical he can be about the quality of food and service and how much he enjoys being treated like a celebrity at this particular establishment—always warmly greeted by the manager and seated right away. However, you feel ashamed as you walk past people waiting for a table and thought it might be fun to try a new place tonight.

When you suggest the idea, Chris cuts you off, saying, "I'm not going to be a guinea pig for some brand-new place where we'll probably have to wait to be seated and who knows what the food is like. Forget it." He brushes by you and announces the time that you should be ready to leave for dinner "as planned."

You watch him as he disappears into the shower. You feel fury rising within you, having been scolded like a child for a perfectly reasonable proposal. You then take a breath and try to see the picture of Chris as a child emerge before you—the one you keep in your wallet, right next to yours. You imagine the little guy in Chris who was never shown how to share, play fair, give and take—the boy who was emasculated by his dad and smothered by his mom. Little Chris was very confused and uncomfortable when it came to relationships and fitting in. You reflect on the image of yourself as a child. She was always afraid of getting yelled at. She did her best to please everyone to avoid disappointing them or feeling guilty. She didn't know what else to do.

You smile inwardly at little Chris and little you, take another calming breath, and say, "Chris, I think we need to talk about what just happened. I know how much you enjoy dining at the Royal Café, being treated nicely, and having your favorite meal prepared just the way you like it. I sometimes feel bad about the people waiting in line while we're seated, but I've had some nice times there with you. You could have explained your feelings to me when I proposed a change. I don't appreciate being cut off and dismissed. I'm simply requesting that we try something different. I agree that the new place may not be a great last-minute choice. But couldn't we be a little adventurous? Can we find a plan that works for both of us? What do you think?"

Chris, who has made no eye contact with you up until now, peers out from the shower and cynically says, "If you know how much I like our usual plan, why do I need a new adventure?" He returns to his shower.

Without missing a beat, you reply, "Chris, I'd really appreciate it if you'd look at me when you're talking to me, as I do with you. I'd like to receive the same courtesy that you expect from me." Chris steps out of the shower, wrapping a towel around his waist. You continue: "Thank you. I'm happy to consider your wishes, and I'd like the same from you. This is a two-way street. I'm merely proposing some give-and-take when it comes to how we spend time together. For this relationship to work, we both need to feel like we matter, like our feelings, opinions, and desires are heard and considered. It sometimes feels like there are different rules for each of us, and that isn't acceptable."

With a less exasperated tone, Chris says, "Okay, I get it. We can talk about it. But please, just not this weekend. I promise we can try something new next time. I just don't feel prepared to do it tonight." You thank him for hearing you and commit to holding him to his promise.

There is no actual apology in this scene. Chris offers a simple acknowledgment and makes a promise. You aren't sure he really got it. But he responds in a gentler tone, with eye contact. The emphasis here is on your proposal for fairness, reciprocity, and taking turns. Moving forward, the yardstick for measuring progress is whether he keeps his word without begrudging you. You may have to follow up and reiterate the importance of getting your needs met in the relationship. You may have to express disappointment if he fails to remember and returns to his self-centered policies. You may have to remind him of what's at stake if he doesn't take this seriously.

Promoting Optimal Awareness by Providing Positive Feedback

While preparing for the annual holiday dinner at your house, your narcissistic brother, Rick, calls to wish you a good holiday and say he'll be a little late. Usually, he either doesn't call when he's running late or says something like, "Listen, I'm running late. I don't know why you have to plan dinner so early. You're so uptight and ridiculous, Susan." Click. However, this time he says, "Hi, Susan. I know this might seem like my typical pattern, and I'm sorry to hold up dinner for everyone, but due to some unforeseen problems here at home, I'll be about twenty minutes late. Is there anything I can bring?"

You immediately think, *Wrong number? He's fallen on his head?* But then you gather yourself and say, "Gee, thanks, Rick. I hope everything is okay. I appreciate your thoughtfulness in calling, and I'd love for you to bring along a couple of extra serving spoons, please. Thanks for asking." You realize this is truly a first. You've spent many years seeding this relationship with honest communication and nourishing it with empathic confrontation, and you're finally seeing the fruits of your labor. You say, "You know, Rick, I'm really grateful for the efforts you're making to be more considerate of me. It really makes me feel closer to you. Thanks again."

He says, "Yeah, I am trying. This would have been a real problem for us in the past. Thanks for noticing."

Offering positive feedback when appropriate is as important as confronting bad behavior. Yes, Rick is late again. He may still have issues with time management, but he's making a noticeable effort to be responsible and thoughtful in his actions. You've been tilling this soil with him for a long time, utilizing your complete set of tools. Pointing out the positive—his thoughtful efforts and simple acts of kindness—is exactly what you need to do to help him feel lovable for his ordinary humanness, not his success and expensive cars.

In this scene, you didn't overstate your appreciation or use words like "wonderful" or "perfect." You didn't refer to his extraordinary job, car, or vocabulary, as you might have in the past, to get his attention or keep him in a good mood. You just offered a simple recognition and a thank-you for being conscious and fairly considerate. Remember, for the narcissist to feel comfortable and connected in relationships, he must learn what he never learned as a child: underneath the bulky layers of glitz and gloss, he is fine as he is. When tenderness, love, and acceptance replace fleeting adulation, he won't feel the need to prove anything or maintain top billing on the marquee.

Integrating an Essential Element: The Raw Truth

You arrive home after another jam-packed day of presentations and staff meetings. This has been one of your most challenging weeks at work ever. After greeting your husband, Ed, with a hug, you say that you'd really appreciate some time to work out and work off some stress before dinner. He says, "Sure, whatever." But you notice his face contorts, suggesting a rising irritation. Before you can inquire, he says, "You know, Karen, I'm sick of your selfishness, and I'm sick of that stupid job of yours. Why don't you just quit and find something else to do? I have had it with the late dinners and your obsessive working out. I don't need this crap anymore. I have more important things to do than sit around waiting for you. There are people who would give anything to be with me. What do I look like, an idiot?" He stares intensely at you.

You're stunned and think, *Here he goes again.* You feel heat surging through your chest, splotching your neck, reddening your face. You may feel like screaming, running to another room to cry, or apologizing. Remember: fight, flight, or freeze. But instead, you pause, breathe, and take a reading on your emotions to see if you can give them a steady and earnest voice without succumbing to those typical responses. If you're too upset to be empathically confrontational, take some time to calm yourself and connect with the present moment before returning to the scene. (I'll discuss time-outs later in this chapter.) Self-possessed, you look Ed in the eye, fully aware of the little boy within who struggled with feelings of loneliness and unworthiness. You summon your recollections of the little girl in you who had such a difficult time asserting herself and trusting her own feelings.

Then, in a calm voice, you say, "Ed, I know how difficult it can be for you to tell me that you miss me. When I'm distracted, like this week, you often feel as if you're unimportant to me. I can understand how upsetting that must be for you. But there's no need to put me down or blame my job. You make it difficult to care about you when you speak to me that way. When you get angry and threaten me, it only causes me to feel hurt and agitated. Your feelings mean a lot to me. But we cannot have a productive discussion if you won't acknowledge your own feelings. I'd like to start this conversation over. How about you?"

Ed looks at you in disbelief. You didn't run away, fight back, or give in. This disarms him momentarily. Then, as his mistrust and discomfort settle back in, he says, "Don't tell me how I feel. I already told you. And, by the way, I have a right to be angry."

You can see the little boy within Ed, stomping his foot, crossing his arms, and secretly wishing that his mom or dad would hold him and take the pain away. You sense his protective armor, but the timbre of his voice has changed. Although his words underscore his anger, he seems to be more engaged with you, as if prompting you to reinforce the message. You move toward him and reply, "Listen, Ed, I get that you feel angry. But the way you express it only pushes me away. I don't think you really want to push me away. I think you want me to hear you and to love you. I'm only asking that you look behind the anger and tell me about the hurt that's also there. It's me. It's safe." You reach to take his hand.

He says in a slightly whiny but gentler tone, "Listen, Karen, I know it's been a tough week for you. But it's tough for me too. I feel a bit useless around here since my consulting job has slowed down, that's all. I get bored and you're rarely ever available these days. [He hangs his head.] Go do your workout. I'll be fine."

You're so pleased. You've reached him. You've extracted the little boy from underneath the mask of the fire-breathing dragon. You have wrapped your brain around his vulnerability, as well as your own. It takes tremendous courage to stand up to a dragon wielding only raw truth. You thank Ed for listening and acknowledge his feelings. You offer to do a shorter workout and propose that the two of you spend some extra time together tonight. He offers a brief smile and an eye roll (still uncomfortable with this type of realness) and accepts your offer.

You may see this as enabling bad behavior by not punishing Ed in some way or ensuring that he deals with consequences. You may feel like you could never say something like that and really mean it when the narcissist is being so insensitive. And you may think, *Who needs to put up with that? Just leave him.* In fact, all of these perspectives may be accurate. Sometimes a relationship with a narcissist is so eroded that the best thing you can do for yourself is to set limits or exit the relationship. Perhaps, you've served generous portions of empathic confrontation but haven't seen any results. Or you may be so wounded that you simply don't have the strength or desire to engage in this process. If so, that's okay. There's no right or wrong decision; there are choices and consequences—and no easy solutions when you're dealing with a narcissist. But if you're reading this book, chances are you've chosen, for now, to stay connected with the narcissist in your life. Once you can integrate mindful awareness with self-advocacy, you'll find that the empathic confrontation approach often leads to more satisfying results, even if it's simply witnessing your own healthy voice rising to the foreground, accurately representing your feelings, rights, and needs. It's you standing up for you, and you can take pleasure in this new experience—the strength of this grounded and loving inner advocate, reminding you of your worth.

Creating Leverage for Change

Earlier I mentioned that it's very difficult to achieve change in your relationship with a narcissist without leverage. In the preceding scenes, the implication that the relationship could collapse creates that leverage. These are relationships of importance: spouse or romantic partner, in-laws and siblings. In these relationships, both parties have chosen to stay connected to each other, and the leverage is that the narcissist doesn't want to lose you. Therefore, there is no need to create leverage by threatening the narcissist, which could result in ugliness and dismissiveness. Instead, create leverage by emphasizing how much the relationship means to you and conveying your fear (or certainty) that it will fall apart if you don't collaborate on making it better, or if he doesn't get professional help. Let's look at three important tools for enhancing leverage in your relationship: the implicit assumption rule, the micro to macro approach, and time-outs.

The Implicit Assumption Rule

The implicit assumption rule is also known as giving someone the benefit of the doubt. You suggest the narcissist doesn't appreciate how hurtful his words are and that he probably didn't mean to be so critical, but that you're upset and it's not acceptable. Remember, most narcissists don't really intend to harm. This is not the motivational driver behind their betrayals, stonewalling, aggressions, gaslighting, and criticalness. Their motivation is to protect their ego at any cost—even if it means hurting you. Nonetheless, it does hurt and they must be held accountable. You can maintain leverage and avoid destructive arguments if you preface your statements with generosity of faith in the narcissist's goodwill, before confronting and setting limits. You want to be heard, yes? Offering the benefit of the doubt implicitly assumes understanding and can manage the narcissist's emotional barometer, warding off defensiveness and counterattacks.

The Micro to Macro Approach

The micro to macro approach (also known as a dress rehearsal) is preparation for living in the world. Despite the narcissist's protestations that he doesn't care what people think of him, the therapist knows that being liked and accepted by others is desirable to all of us, especially the narcissist. Unfavorable behaviors in the treatment room represent a microcosm of his relationships with important others and with the world at large.

You can also use this approach. You can empathically point out that entitled and self-aggrandizing behavior is understandable because you're aware of the confusing messages he received as a child: one moment he was spoiled, the next, deprived and ignored. You tell him you know he seeks to gain status by ignoring the rules and expecting special attention. Then you explain that, while you've worked hard to understand him and care enough to be open with him and even forgiving, others may see him as unpleasant or arrogant, and not care enough to tell him the truth.

He may counter with a raised eyebrow and phrases like, "Oh, give me a break, people respect me," or "If you could just learn to listen and be a little more appreciative like my team at work," or "You know, nothing I do is good enough for you." You follow with, "Yes, you have a lot of admiration for your achievements, and that's well-earned. But people listen because they are intimidated and fearful. They don't want to lose their jobs or the perks of being associated with you. This is not the same as choosing to be with you, respecting you, or feeling good when in your presence."

This enhances your leverage because he can't hide from your compassion and soothing wisdom, and he fears the pain of perpetual exclusion.

Time-Outs

To maintain leverage with the narcissist, you need to be heard. If you're angry and at the threshold of a toxic verbal discharge or withdrawal, you may need time to de-escalate your feelings and deconstruct the events that pushed your buttons. This will help you maximize your potential for being heard. Self-help books for dealing with anger are chock-full of suggestions to take a time-out when flooded with overwhelming feelings or intense anger. This is good advice. Time-outs can be very helpful for de-escalation, self-reflection, and allowing the fight, flight, or freeze response to subside.

John Gottman, an internationally known expert in relationships and predictors of divorce, discusses the challenges and importance of calming the heart and the nervous system before engaging in healing communication after a rupturing episode (Gottman and Silver 2004). He points out that while many well-adjusted and reportedly happy couples can fight without harming their relationship, couples who have a fragile connection fight in damaging ways and often need time to stabilize their turbulent emotional and physiological states before entering the repair zone.

The time-out is often defined as each person seeking some temporary distance from the other, perhaps by going to another room or taking a walk for some negotiated amount of time. The idea is to have a cooling-off period before revisiting the dispute or even just being around each other. In schema therapy, we also recommend that when you're triggered and flooded with overwhelming or angry sensations, it's best to seek a temporary refuge to catch your breath and regain your emotional equilibrium. But what can you do to help you get comfortable in your own skin again, to help you become sturdy and effective in the next round of engagement?

BREATHE

Those gentle, calming breaths you use in your mindfulness practice (described in chapter 5) can be helpful. During a time-out, dedicate a few moments to feeling the rise and fall of your abdomen, your lungs expanding and contracting, the coolness of the air you inhale, and the warmth of your exhalation. With each breath, bathe your mind and body in lulling tranquility and vibrant clarity.

USE A SCHEMA FLASH CARD

Keep a flash card or two that can help you identify the schema you've fallen prey to and awaken you to the present. The flash card, much like the ones you or your children may have used for memorizing math problems and vocabulary words, can be an index card, a piece of paper, or a note on your smartphone. It can also be an audio file you record for yourself. The flash card guides you toward healthier responses using the four steps you learned in chapter 4 (observe, assess, identify, and differentiate). You then add a final step—finding healthy ways to soothe yourself:

1. **Observe:** Notice the feelings you're experiencing.

2. **Assess:** Link the corresponding schemas to these feelings, as well as to your reactions.

3. **Identify:** Label the feelings and responses that may be schema driven.

4. **Differentiate:** Let go of the phantoms of the past and notice yourself from a here-and-now perspective.

5. **Self-soothe:** Look for healthy ways to soothe yourself in the present moment.

Here's how that might look:

1. *I'm aware that I'm feeling furious with the narcissist.*

2. *My emotional deprivation and self-sacrifice schemas are activated because I feel misunderstood and resent being taken for granted.*

3. *I want to scream and punish him. I also notice food cravings.*

4. *These are the feelings of the powerless little girl who had to make tremendous sacrifices to feel appreciated and noticed. But I don't need to prove anything now. I have choices. I'm not powerless, and I have rights in this relationship. Spewing anger at the narcissist is useless. This just reminds him that I am still in his game. Bingeing on unhealthy foods may be soothing momentarily, but it can only camouflage my pain, not heal it. I have a right to feel angry, but I don't need to become the anger. I am a capable adult who understands the narcissist's issues as well as my own. I can be an effective spokesperson for my feelings and a good advocate for my vulnerable self. I must advocate for myself without acting out.*

5. *Instead of flipping into angry mode or suppressing my feelings with food, I could do something else:*

   - *Write in my journal for five minutes.*

   - *Call my friend who always knows how to calm and reassure me.*

   - *Practice what I'd like to communicate and how I'll say it when we take the issue up again.*

ENGAGE IN DISTRACTION

Healthy distractions can also be valuable for stabilizing your mood and calming your emotions while in time-out mode. Here are some suggestions:

- Read or write poetry.

- Listen to music.

- Do a crossword puzzle.

- Organize.

- Make a to-do list.

- Dance or sing.

- Exercise.

- Meditate.

- Take a bath.

- Get a massage.

Empathy and the Therapy Relationship: Finding the Right Therapist

Many partners and family members of narcissists ask me, "What happens in therapy with a narcissist? How do I find the right therapist? What should I be looking for in a therapist, and what's the most effective approach for treating narcissism?"

1. The therapist shouldn't simply listen and validate the narcissist's complaints and avoidance. The therapist must be firm and able to withstand the narcissist's anger or criticism. If the therapist is too passive, the narcissist will probably waste time showing off, blaming, seeking approval, and possibly taunting the therapist. If the therapist is intimidated, the narcissist will sense it, seek to dominate the therapist, and hijack therapy or end it. And while the therapist must be knowledgeable about narcissism, she must be more than an expert in theory; she must be authentic. If the therapist is too intellectual, there's a risk she will reinforce the narcissist's competitive and detached coping modes.

2. The therapist must also have an authentic curiosity, and be able to express empathy, understanding, and self-disclosure to elicit emotional resonance. This means experiencing the internal world of the client, though not necessarily agreeing with him. Indeed, empathic confrontation is one of the most important skills in treating these clients. I often approach narcissistic clients saying things like, "Yes, I get that your dad gave you the message

that you were entitled to special privileges, but the world doesn't work that way. Your dad didn't prepare you to live in this world, especially taking responsibility for the impact of your reactions on others and allowing yourself to be truly loved. And the way you're speaking to me right now is very off-putting and distracting. I imagine it must be hard for people to hear you when they're distracted by this offensive tone."

3. In therapy, empathic awareness is the launching pad for setting limits and holding clients accountable. Sometimes it opens the door to deeper investigations. Pushing against the narcissist's defiant avoidance and emotional detachment can help alter self-defeating patterns and intolerable emotions that have kept him stuck.

4. The therapist must be able to tell the truth, even when it means setting limits, and also be mindful, operating in and reflecting moment-to-moment experiences in the therapy relationship. Narcissists have a lot of mistrust, especially of people who claim to care about them. They feel these people just want something from them, and that they are being used or manipulated as in early life. Illuminating the truth creates a bond that allows for safety and trust in the therapeutic relationship. Ultimately, the therapist must be capable of telling the truth to a narcissistic client and setting limits without disparaging the client. In this way, the therapist helps reparent the client, enhancing his healthy adult self by meeting the core needs of the vulnerable part buried within.

5. Finally, having intermittent contact with a partner (if there is a partner) can be critical to effective treatment outcomes. Partners can offer valuable feedback to the therapist as progress is evaluated. Partners can also benefit from the therapist coaching them with strategies that, in a modified way, mimic what is happening

in treatment, and thus keep new patterns alive in the midsession days. Eventually, the therapist may see the couple together to address issues of trust, finances, faith, fidelity, intimacy repair, co-parenting, and perhaps crafting a vision for the future.

Conclusion

Change can be an arduous and exasperating undertaking. Not everyone is ready or willing to change. Fear can be a primary obstacle, including fear of dreadful feelings embedded in our schemas, even if the goal is to assuage those feelings. But given all that you've learned, you know that change is possible, and you may feel hopeful. In this chapter, you've had a chance to see that possibility in action. You've sampled some of the most crucial implements for inspiring change: empathic confrontation, sturdy self-advocacy, setting limits, and maintaining leverage. Next, we will look at ways you might implement some of these strategies (and more) when co-parenting with a narcissist.

CHAPTER 8

Co-Parenting with a Narcissist: *Protecting Your Children and Supporting Their Wellness*

There are only two lasting bequests we can hope to give our children. One of these is roots, the other, wings.

—Johann Wolfgang von Goethe

Parenting may be one of the most challenging, meaningful, wearying, and rewarding jobs we can undertake as adults, even when two parents are working in synchrony, sharing the joys and the burdens. We choose someone to have children with, expecting to share responsibility with a sensitive and beloved ally, a best friend, an emotionally intelligent co-parenting compatriot who will share our values and forgive our stumbles. As in the beautiful quote by Goethe, we hope to be able to ground our children with a sense of belonging while simultaneously encouraging them to discover their natural inclinations and develop autonomy—to find their wings.

But, sadly, some of you have discovered that your co-parenting compatriot, your children's father or mother, is actually one of the most narcissistically demanding, controlling, bullying, entitled, or simply hands-off and disconnected, people in your life. And still, you need to find a way to effectively co-parent with this person. You will need to navigate around the narcissistic imperatives, such as self-righteousness and attention seeking, while dodging inexplicable rage stemming from low impulse control. It's a lot to endure, and an often lonely endeavor.

Co-parenting with a narcissist requires a sturdy sense of self, whether living with your co-parent or in separate homes. You will need to avoid spending your precious energy enduring his temper tantrums, argumentativeness, boundary-breaking violations, and gaslighting. You will need to speak clearly and firmly, enforce boundaries, and set limits. You will need to cultivate and care for the healthiest you possible to undertake the exhausting "repair work" that ensures your children's self-esteem, prepares them for a satisfying interpersonal life, fosters a secure attachment to the world, and buoys their confidence as they develop autonomy.

Dan Siegel and Mary Hartzell offer hope and inspiration, observing that children can become resilient and compassionate when they have at least one parent who offers their child a healthy best self. Your greatest gift to your child is not being perfect; it's being healthy, which includes being someone who can repair ruptures caused by both you and the co-parenting narcissist. You're only human, after all.

Together or Apart: Common Scenarios

So, let's dive into the nitty gritty of how you might vigorously address the damaging behaviors of the narcissistic co-parent, in order to nurture and protect the welfare of your children. I will continue to use the male pronoun, but please know that these issues are gender-neutral and the strategies can be applied to both female and male narcissistic co-parents.

Additionally, while there are some differences between co-parenting with the narcissist together in one home and co-parenting from separate homes, in both cases the *offended* co-parents will report concerns. The most common of these concerns are reflected in the following questions:

1. How do I protect my child from becoming a narcissist like his father? What are the signs?

2. How do I get my narcissistic co-parent to stop belittling me in front of the children and to stop overriding my decisions?

3. How do I get my narcissistic co-parent to model safety and healthy distress tolerance, including wearing a seat belt, no drinking and driving, monitoring children's exposure to inappropriate material, setting limits on screen time and unhealthy foods, patiently waiting their turn in line, and being respectful toward people assisting them?

4. How do I get my narcissistic co-parent to ease up on the expectations and demands he places on the children, including the constant need for perfection and the degrading critical or cold-shouldered responses given when the children do not meet his expectations? My son is beginning to have angry outbursts and is becoming more critical of himself when he makes a mistake or doesn't score the winning goal.

5. How do I handle my narcissistic co-parent bad-mouthing me to my children when I'm not present? My children reluctantly share

this with me, fearing repercussions if I confront their (narcissis-tic) parent.

6. How do I deal with the barrage of threats that I will "lose access to my children," "lose support," or "lose my children's love" if I don't fall in line with my narcissistic co-parent's demands?

7. How do I get my narcissistic co-parent to engage more lovingly, patiently, playfully, and emotionally with the children—to be present, empathize with their feelings, and express acceptance?

8. How might I encourage my narcissistic co-parent to get profes-sional parenting help, allow the children to receive therapy, or enter family therapy?

9. How do I explain narcissism to my children? Is this even a good idea?

Some of the chief concerns when living apart, in addition to the obvious inability to consistently observe and supervise the actions or inactions of your narcissistic co-parent, might include these:

10. How do I get my narcissistic co-parent to follow the visitation and shared custody agreement? He is always late picking up/drop-ping off our children, shows up at my home without notice, and expects me to modify the schedule for him at a moment's notice.

11. How can I effectively communicate concerns regarding the chil-dren to my narcissistic co-parent? Every time I try, he gets angry and hangs up or just blows me off and walks away.

12. How do I address the issue of my children having premature exposure to my narcissistic co-parent's dating relationships and overnight guests?

13. How do I deal with what appears to be my narcissistic co-parent's abuse of the children? My children tell me that they are fearful

and hurt, or they are acting out because of emotional or physical bullying by the narcissist. (This one may also pertain to those living with the narcissistic co-parent.)

IMPORTANT: In the event of any threat to your children's safety—high-risk or dangerous activity, physical or sexual harm—immediately seek the assistance of a local or national domestic violence program, a lawyer, a family therapist, the police department, a family crisis intervention service, or child protective services in your location. If you don't know where to turn for help, contact the National Domestic Violence Hotline at 1-800-799-7233.

Prosocial Strategies for Co-Parenting with a Narcissist

Please remember that when dealing with a narcissist, your challenges are greater than the average co-parenting struggles, change is slow and may not always be possible, and there are no perfect outcomes. But you can still raise children who feel loved, competent, and grounded by your presence. Best-selling author and parenting expert, Susan Stiffelman, and I have cohosted a monthly online support and education community dedicated to co-parenting with a narcissist. Susan reminds everyone that it takes one healthy parent to raise a well-adjusted and emotionally secure child into a healthy, self-actualized adult.

Prosocial strategies, including empathic confrontation, emphasize the notion of cooperation, helpfulness, problem-solving, and rule-following (an antonym for narcissism). Prosocial behaviors inspire our children to find their place among their fellow humans, garnering self-respect and other-respect, and working well with others. In the next pages, I'll give you targeted strategies to address each of the concerns reflected in the questions above. Read through each strategy, and choose the suggestions that fit your specific situation, adapting them as needed so that you feel empowered to provide your children with opportunities to thrive.

Supporting Healthy Emotional Growth (Concern 1)

Having a narcissistic co-parent who models short-temperedness and entitlement, makes unreasonable demands, and judges you (or others) in harsh ways can set the stage for the child to mimic the actions and attitudes of that parent, especially when the parent is also the identified gender role model.

However, a child who receives unconditional love and acceptance—who feels seen and understood; safe, respected, encouraged and supported; and who is able to learn how to tolerate frustration and reasonable limits—will be on a path toward emotionally, physically, and interpersonally prospering in the world.

STRATEGY 1: USE "PARTS" LANGUAGE

Discuss with your child how "we all have parts of us that can behave in ways that are not helpful and are even hurtful sometimes, and your dad has this part in him too. He has parts of him that can be loving, fun, athletic, and very smart when helping you with tough math problems, but he also has a part that gets upset easily, and that says and does things that can be hurtful, even when he doesn't mean to."

This approach, which avoids any (albeit tempting) bad-mouthing of the narcissistic co-parent, fortifies healthy modeling and imitation, and prevents any perceived alienation from the narcissistic co-parent. You might also prevent mimicry of negative patterns with keen attention to modeling healthy actions, attitudes, and reactions, and educating your child about the value of patience, fairness, equanimity, and kindness. Remind your child that their narcissistic parent's behaviors are not the child's fault: "He is the grown-up. This is his problem and no one else's. This is certainly not a way to be, even though I know how much you would like to be like the other positive parts of your dad."

STRATEGY 2: MAINTAIN BALANCE

Express praise for your children's everyday courtesies—their thought-fulness, playfulness, curiosity, creativity, sharing of emotion and ideas about how the world works—balanced by praise for their efforts in school, sports, performing arts, or even how they strive to make a good appearance.

Set limits and remember that discipline is not a dirty word, especially when expressed in a loving and reasonably flexible way. We all come to appreciate the value of having survived the discomfort of taking turns, having to wait, or stopping play and attending to homework. Allow your children to make (safe) mistakes so they can realize they are still lovable and acceptable, even if their actions were not acceptable.

Believe in them, offer support, and encourage them to keep trying when they struggle. Empathize with their experiences and beliefs without judgment of their character or their worth.

STRATEGY 3: CONFRONT EMPATHICALLY

Remind the narcissistic co-parent how important and powerful his role is in the life of his child. Point out that his child looks up to him, and while he may have many admirable traits, there are parts of him that may confuse and compromise his child's best outcome: "C'mon Joe, you're a smart guy and you love Christopher. I know you don't mean to make him feel like he has to be tough to win you over. Surely you can see how your anger and criticalness might be showing up in how he treats his sister and the way he acts out in school."

When the narcissist responds snarkily, take comfort in knowing that you planted a seed and that it may be enough to get his attention, because it makes sense. You let him know that you are watching, even if he doesn't acknowledge it and continues to be critical of you.

Encouraging Respect and Cooperation (Concern 2)

This is challenging, especially when the narcissist undermines your disciplinary measures. It is essential to construct a parenting agreement that is sensitive to the needs of your children and that focuses on how to embolden values, enforce discipline, and inspire good habits. But this can be a hard-won battle, even between two relatively healthy adults.

A narcissist may change the rules to suit himself, and, given his lack of impulse control and need for everything to be on his terms, he may also scold and belittle you in front of your children. Children, hence, become confused and burdened with having to choose. They, of course, want to choose the path of least discomfort, even if it's not particularly favorable to their welfare. Your children might choose the path that stops the fighting by trying to abort the conflict and appease the narcissist so he calms down. It's hard to watch your children bear the burden and forfeit their vulnerability to stop the drama and make the narcissist feel vindicated. They may even join the narcissist in scolding and blaming you. But even in the face of this harsh reality, continue to model respect and cooperation.

STRATEGY 1: DISENGAGE AND DEPART

Exit the conversation. Simply and calmly say, "We can discuss this in private."

STRATEGY 2: USE "WE" PHRASES

Find a quiet, private moment to confront the narcissistic co-parent about your concerns regarding how "we" argue in front of the children. Discuss what you would like, such as communicating with respect and acknowledging the love you "both" have for your children.

While it can feel utterly unfair, narcissists respond best to the "we" phrases, which deflect their knee-jerk defensiveness. You might begin with something like this: "I am sure you probably noticed Doug's face and his confusion and distress last night when we were in dispute about signing him up for another competitive sport. We must be careful to hold those disagreements for private moments when we can talk and come to a joint conclusion, even if it's a compromise, without exposing him to the struggle. Could we perhaps have a code word or a way to flag each other when we see that we are approaching conflict so that we might stop and discuss it alone later?"

Pause. Breathe. Allow your narcissistic co-parent to respond, or to roll his eyes, or perhaps both. Then calmly continue: "I know we don't see eye to eye on this, and I appreciate your enthusiasm for his love of sports. But we did have an agreement about this, yes? I am sure you can also see the wisdom in my concern for his already overloaded schedule and his desire for a little downtime. I think he so wants to please you that he fears ever letting you see his weariness. That's not your fault, nor his. He wants to emulate you and your athletic performance, so the burden for both of you becomes great. I think we can figure this out together and help him have a healthy and happy fall, maintain his schoolwork, and get enough rest, without judging or demeaning one another, especially in front of him. I assume you did not mean to be hurtful, nor do you want your son to disrespect me, but it was hurtful. He copies you to make peace and win your approval. That's a lot for a little guy to manage, and I know you agree because you had a similar burden, didn't you?"

This may, again, be met with a dismissive glare, a snarling comment, or a complete shutdown of your point of view—or, perhaps, a quiet acceptance or even a few words of agreement. While the latter is always a treat, the goal is to be heard, to drop those precious seeds into the soil, and to watch for possible harvesting of new behaviors.

Reference this conversation when the rupture happens again and commit to not engage when it happens in front of your child. Don't attack, threaten, or demand. This will only fire up the narcissist's love of the contest—a guaranteed dead end. Be sure to start with what you don't want: a fight about who's right and who's wrong.

Modeling Safety, Respect, and Healthy Limits (Concern 3)

This is not easy. Getting the narcissistic co-parent to be a better model—follow safety guidelines, tolerate reasonable limits and frustrations, be respectful toward others—is a colossal challenge. Because the narcissist claims that he always knows best, he cannot be told what to do and must always be in charge. Therefore, you must employ strategies that both seek to compensate for his underlying insecurities and provide a healthy model for your children.

STRATEGY 1: BE THE *GOOD ENOUGH* MODEL

No parent is perfect. However, do your best to model behaviors that are the opposite of what your children may witness and experience with the narcissistic parent. Using "parts" language (as described above) helps alleviate confusion about their parents' differing behaviors.

Notice and model ordinary acts of kindness and tolerance. Give positive feedback to your children when they show tolerance and respect, and when they exhibit wise actions, such as when they buckle their seat belt without being asked. Recognize them when they're cooperative, even if they aren't pleased—for example, about having to end their play time. Appreciate their offer to help a sibling or their willingness to attend to their studies.

STRATEGY 2: EXPRESS EMPATHY

Empathize with your children's disappointment and struggle, and reinforce their ability to rise above it. Enforce thoughtful, not punitive, consequences to empower them to see and make choices. Choices and consequences help prepare your children for life. (This is something the narcissist has learned to bypass, until held accountable with meaningful stakes.)

STRATEGY 3: USE EMPATHIC CONFRONTATION FOR LIMIT SETTING

When addressing dangerous risk-taking behaviors with the narcissist, stand firm while invoking the benefit-of-the doubt approach. Here's an example:

Empathy: "I know you're accustomed to doing as you please and not answering to anyone, especially at work where you're in charge of other people and make rapid decisions. You're good at it too.

Confrontation: "But parenting, as you know, is an important responsibility—for both of us—and I know we both want our children to feel safe, loved, and competent. Not wearing seat belts or drinking and driving [fill in the dangerous behavior here] is not acceptable for either of us. We are both models and guardians of our children."

Empathy: "I know this may feel like I am telling you what to do, and that's triggering for you. You may also feel angry or frustrated with me. However, I am no longer willing to tolerate the, albeit unintentional, harmful consequences these actions can cause our children. This is nonnegotiable, Joe."

Confrontation: The narcissistic co-parent may smugly reply, "Yeah, so what are you going to do about it?" If he does, be prepared with a meaningful and actionable consequence, even if it means going so far as to propose legal intervention, family therapy, or contacting child protective services to assess parental guidelines and limits for child safety.

STRATEGY 4: MAINTAIN A STURDY SELF

You can also ask the narcissist, "What would you have me do? If you were concerned about my actions posing safety risks to the children, what would you do to protect them?" This usually stops the narcissist in his tracks and he harrumphs off. Or he may offer an angry litany of reasons that you're not a good parent.

Try to avoid the temptation to defend yourself, especially when you have nothing to defend. This is the old bait, the predictable game. Don't fall into this old pattern. Instead, show interest in his concerns concerning the impact of your behavior on the children's well-being, and agree to discuss proposals for how the two of you might reach common ground.

The narcissist will not go much further with this, because his intention was to intimidate you into backing off and to lord it over all decisions. But you are a steel rod of fortitude now, for both yourself and your children. You will not shrink or fold. You may need to repeat this new voice, this new stance. It may even, in some cases, require legal intervention.

STRATEGY 5: TEACH EMPOWERMENT AND ASSERTIVENESS

Validate your children's feelings and encourage them to express sadness, fears, and worries about their narcissistic parent. The narcissistic parent may blame you for their upset and worry. Help your children employ the "parts" strategy, and enable them to anticipate responses from their narcissistic parent to their distress.

You might role-play a dialogue with them, encouraging them to maintain authenticity without defensiveness, using strategies like empathic confrontation. Nine-year-old Charlotte told her narcissistic dad, "I know you love me, Daddy, and I love spending some time with you, but not when you drive fast and without your seat belt. It scares me and makes me feel unsafe." Dad says, "Oh, what, did your mom tell you to say that?" Little Charlotte replies, "No, she just told me it was okay to let you know how I feel." Bravo, Charlotte.

Protecting Your Child from Unhealthy Influence (Concern 4)

Sadly, many a vainglorious co-parent relies on his children (or chosen child) to reflect his image, a representation of his mastery and triumph, a trophy on behalf of his needy ego. Alternatively, the narcissistic co-parent may relate to his child as a rival for attention in a high-stakes competition for agility, beauty, and academic accomplishments. The narcissistic co-parent can (unknowingly) initiate such contests with his child. He may then turn away from this child, or engage in nitpicky fault finding whenever the child shows pride in their proficiency or enjoys a compliment.

Whether it's high expectations and unyielding demands for excellence, harsh criticisms, or (conversely) jealousy-driven coldness when the child captures the spotlight, these are tough, confusing messages and difficult experiences for your child. You, the healthy parent, will have to work hard to spare your child from the emotional scar tissue formed by unrealistic demands, hurtful criticisms, or emotional neglect. However, because your child has a memory, you may not be able to prevent all scars, but you can reduce their impact and keep them from becoming a damaging early maladaptive schema.

STRATEGY 1: NURTURE, EDUCATE, AND MODEL

Holding, hugs, and snuggles can be an affirming and assuring means for connection and security. And when you feel frustrated, model a "pause"—breathe deep, stretch, gather your thoughts, and start over. By doing so, you will help your children learn a healthy coping strategy for regulating emotions and sensations when they're under pressure and endeavoring to make themselves heard.

Carefully offering knowledge about narcissism and personality problems—as you have done for yourself—reduces the intensity and impact on your children when it comes to self-blame, shame, and personalization of their narcissistic co-parent's behaviors.

STRATEGY 2: BE A RECEPTIVE LISTENER AND SAFE REFUGE

Make space for listening with compassion. Allow your children to vent their frustrations. Don't rush in with problem-solving, and be mindful not to double their burden by joining them in the chorus of complaints about their narcissistic parent.

Be a safe refuge and neutral space where they can share their sadness, fear, angst, and fury. Listen, hold, and soothe them with a gentle, empathic, "I know." Then ask, "Is there more?" Answer questions if asked, but be careful not to allow your fear to trap you into making a promise that you cannot keep, such as, "You don't ever have to [see your dad…, talk to your mom about…, go to your sports practice…, go with Dad to the…] again."

Once they're shared their difficult emotions, you might do a fun and familiar ritual, something you've come up with together, such as playing outside, doing a puzzle, dancing to music, cooking together, or going for a bike ride.

STRATEGY 3: USE BENEFIT OF THE DOUBT

When confronting the narcissistic co-parent, use this strategy. Accentuate the word "important" and offer benefit of the doubt: "I imagine you may be concerned, and perhaps you have been wanting to discuss Little Johnny's sleepovers as well…"

Narcissists are drawn to words and phrases that assume they are intelligent and "good guys." Remind the narcissistic co-parent that he possesses a unique power to influence his child's sense of personal value and self-esteem. You might also remind the narcissist, with empathy, what you imagine his childhood was like (especially if he had a harsh and demanding parent or a rivalrous one).

STRATEGY 4: USE VOICE-RECORDED MESSAGES

Whether living together or apart, but especially when apart, consider scripting your message, recording it with your phone, and sending it to your narcissistic co-parent. He can listen at his convenience and without interrupting you with counterattacks. Include an invitation to discuss this further, indicating your interest in hearing his point of view.

Striving for Balance (Concern 5)

At the severe end of the spectrum, narcissists gaslight their children in order to manipulate the children's attachment to you or to try to alienate them from you by bad-mouthing and blaming you. This might be retaliation for a divorce, or, at the moderate point on the spectrum, it could be an attempt to win the children's favor when the two of you are in conflict.

It's about who wins and who loses, who's right and who's wrong. The narcissist must always be the righteous winner because, for him, the alternative is unbearable. Remember, being seen as the "bad guy" or the "failure" is the monster in the narcissist's closet. Your challenge in the face of the narcissist's rigid black-white approach to parenting is to strive to maintain a steady, balanced, and flexible stance so that your children feel free to express their distress, without fear of judgment or retaliation.

STRATEGY 1: BE THE SAFE PLACE

Your children surreptitiously share with you that their dad has been bad-mouthing you. With tremendous trepidation, they fear the fallout when he discovers what they've disclosed to you. As difficult as this can be, simply empathically listen, comfort, and soothe, as in concern 4. Words like these can quash fear and offer relief: "This must be very hard for you to tell me, honey. I appreciate your courage. You can share anything with me. Do you have any questions for me? Let's have a hug."

You can also empower your children by role-playing ways in which they can let their narcissistic parent know how much this bad-mouthing upsets them, that they don't like it, and that they want it to stop.

STRATEGY 2: USE "WE" STATEMENTS

Confronting the narcissistic co-parent involves a thoughtful posture and careful language, especially when trying to protect a promise to your children of nondisclosure. Again, the "we" phrases can be very useful for *dropping seeds*. You might try something like this: "Despite our differences, and the conflict that we've both endured [or "we are enduring"], let's not let our distress spill into our relationship with the children. They love us both and they need us both. Let's protect their right to feel secure in their attachment to each of us throughout this process. I am committed to that, how about you?"

And when your narcissistic co-parent becomes defensive or suspicious, resist the temptation to take it any further. Just top it off with, "I know it's hard for you to trust my intentions, but I am committed to this effort for their sake and for our mutual well-being too."

Countering the Narcissist's Threats (Concern 6)

The narcissist's hotheaded response to shame, or loss of privilege, entitlement, or status, as we've discussed earlier, is to deny, defend, and blame. He may also threaten retaliatory action when it comes to financial settlements as well as child custody and visitation. It's the old "I'll show you" mantra. However, until the narcissistic co-parent actually acts on his threats, he is usually just blustering for attention, trying to get you to "dance" to the old familiar two-step of (1) you get frightened, and (2) he wins.

Or he wants you to "drop" whatever it is (probably a rightful claim to be upset) that causes him to feel deflated or defamed. He wants you to "act" in some way that allows him to reclaim his sovereignty.

When it comes to financial and child custody/visitation agreements, fair outcomes will not usually prevail in negotiating with a narcissistic co-parent, or at least not perfectly. You stand a decent chance of protecting your rights if you pursue legal advocacy.

STRATEGY 1: USE AFFIRMATIONS

Certain phrases and words can keep you calm and steady in the stormiest of times—for example, "I have rights…," "I will be okay…," "I have support…," or "I am sturdy…" This can also be a good time to pause and set a limit. Literally remove yourself from the barbed monologue of the narcissistic co-parent, and say, "Clearly, this is not going in a productive direction. Surely, even you know that your words are nonsensical. In the spirit of protecting our co-parenting relationship, I am not going to participate in this conversation. Perhaps we can try again later. I am stopping for now."

Keep a clear head and remind yourself, or ask someone close to you to remind you, that you have legal rights. Although divorcing a narcissistic co-parent can be a harrowing process with unwanted compromises, you are not going to "lose everything."

STRATEGY 2: SEEK LEGAL HELP

Consult an attorney (particularly one who specializes in narcissism), and educate yourself about your legal rights. Learn what to anticipate and how to prepare, should you need to pursue legal action to protect yourself and your children. Review the attorney's experience (with examples) of dealing with a narcissist in matters of divorce, financial support, child custody, visitation, and co-parenting decision-making.

IMPORTANT: If the narcissistic co-parent is capable of (or has shown signs of) unsafe, high-risk, or violent behavior, or if he is making threats of abducting your children, consult a domestic violence counselor, a family therapist, an attorney, and/or a child protective services agent immediately. When in imminent danger, contact the police for a court order of protection.

Making an Impact on Behavior and Decision-Making (Concerns 7, 8, and 9)

Some narcissistic co-parents are quite good at nurturing their children, or good at least some of the time. When asked in treatment, they will report that these inclinations feel as if summoned directly from their own vulnerability and memories of unmet emotional needs.

But, sadly, this is not the case for most. While they love their children (in the limited ways narcissists can express love), they are either not emotionally present or not consistently nurturing, especially in emotional engagement. In the worst case, the narcissist unintentionally or intentionally seeks to sculpt his children into what he presumes will grant him status as "parent of the year." This can mean placing harsh and critical demands on the children, overemphasizing performance, subjugating them to a legacy-driven future—"You will join my law firm one day, of course"—or simply emotionally detaching from the children completely and expecting you to engage them in upwardly mobile endeavors and to ensure a winning appearance.

Of course, your children's self-esteem may become a casualty of absent emotional presence or unremitting expectations and critical judgment. Co-parenting therapy, family therapy, and/or child therapy are good options for getting support and guidance to repair such ruptures and to heal a family. But attempting this with a narcissistic co-parent becomes a titanic challenge, much like getting him to seek individual or couple's therapy.

Furthermore, educating your children about issues of narcissism can leave you ill at ease, as you strive to avoid placing additional burdens on your children, bad-mouthing the narcissistic co-parent, and alienating the children from their parent. The strategies below address these important concerns.

STRATEGY 1: USE (EMPATHIC) CONFRONTATION AND LEVERAGE

Toss in those "we" phrases, lest you end up in the counterattack dance again. It may go something like this: "I expect this won't be a favorite notion for either of us, as we have struggled to find common ground and have differing ideas about how best to create self-worth and healthy development for the kids. But it's something you've undoubtedly considered yourself [give credit where credit is not due, but needed]: I think we need to look for some professional coaching [often narcissists can accept this term more easily than "therapy"] to help us with our co-parenting conflict."

You might also add: "I think the children could benefit from some additional support as well. Our differences might be affecting their emotional security as well as their confidence. We may be getting in the way of their focus instead of enhancing it." This tells the narcissist that you are not backing down or compromising your parenting values. You are simply interested in a proposal from a professional. You are also showing concern about your children's ability to maintain a sense of internal comfort and external competence, the latter being of critical importance to the narcissist. Here again you employ leverage—meaningful consequences—to get the narcissist's buy-in.

STRATEGY 2: USE "PARTS" LANGUAGE

Using "parts" language may be your best strategy for helping your children to understand their narcissistic parent. Remind them that life is chock-full of choices and that choices come with consequences: "You know when that part of you gets so upset when your team loses the game—last time, you came home and broke your sister's guitar. Remember? We talked about that part of you that has every right to be upset and disappointed, but does not have the right to take it out on someone else or to destroy property. There were consequences for that, yes? I know it felt like you had no choice, but I see that you are getting much better about expressing your upsets without hurting anyone or anything, and I am so proud of you."

You might add examples of other personality parts, even some of your own: happy parts, worrier-parent parts, silly parts, sometimes-too-serious parts, creative parts, and more. Then you can easily segue into discussing the parts of the narcissistic parent's personality: "Your dad means well. He wants you to have a good life and an even better future than he or his family had. He loves you, but he also has parts of him that can get in the way of that love and can make you feel, as you've said, that you're bad, invisible, or always letting him down. I know this is hurtful, even though he may not wish to hurt you. But it's his responsibility to work on that part of himself, not yours. Only he can make those changes. You have every right to be tired of this, and you have every right to let him know how you feel about it."

Some parents may choose to share "parts" language and other resources with their young adult children as a way to gently help them understand what they are up against with a narcissistic parent. Again, the goal is not to disparage the narcissistic co-parent, but to spare your children from the biased representations of how the interpersonal world works, and from the burden of unwarranted self-blame and subjugation. In age-appropriate language, always reassure them that they are not the cause of their narcissistic parent's negative actions or inactions toward them. Fill that unconditional love reservoir and affectionately remind them that they are lovable and cherished just as they are, even when they make mistakes or have difficult times or careless reactions.

Sharing, Communicating, and Facing Challenges When Living Apart (Concerns 10, 11, 12, and 13)

When living apart (or even sometimes when living together), you may find yourself faced with a narcissist who is quick to anger or to dismiss any communication that may threaten his ego. He can't tolerate feeling that he is being managed or told what to do by anyone, whether that is you or, if living apart, the court system.

Sturdy receptivity fastened with persevering grit will be the winning stance as you pause, breathe, straighten your spine, tuck your vulnerable self into your imagined safe place, and then bypass the explosive emotions and actions of your wounded and irascible narcissistic co-parent. From your healthy, wise, and unflinching co-parenting mode, you emerge as an unstoppable, if weary, advocate for your children. And you will not be ignored when it comes to respect, safety, and stability.

STRATEGY 1: UTILIZE LEGAL INTERVENTIONS AND PROFESSIONAL GUIDANCE

You may already have court-ordered agreements about schedules; pick-up, drop-off, and drop-in arrangements; or dating guidelines—such as the timing for exposing the children to new romantic relationships and the policy for overnight dates during custodial days. Other matters, such as, school, extracurricular activities, tutors, health care, religious studies, and so on, may also be part of the court mandate.

Seeking outside advocacy may be necessary when your narcissistic co-parent disregards or downright violates agreements and/or when your children's welfare is infringed upon or exploited. Contact your lawyer, mediator, family court, or therapist for guidance on how best to proceed. Of course, if your children's physical safety is at risk, you will need to immediately seek to obtain a protective order from the courts.

STRATEGY 2: USE CAREFUL COMMUNICATION AND THOUGHTFUL TIMING

When confronting breaches of agreements, careful communication and thoughtful timing will be your most effective tools. Communication is best done in person, by phone, or by audio/video message. I don't recommend email, text messaging, or other written messages because written messages can easily be misconstrued. They also limit emphasis that only the voice—or voice plus facial/bodily expression—can articulate. Write your communication as a last resort—or in the case of a no-contact agreement.

That said, you know your narcissistic co-parent best, and you may already have a sense of how to most effectively deliver your message. Trust yourself; you can always experiment with another option if your first choice gets derailed.

Timing matters too. You might say something like this: "If this is not a good time, we can choose a time that is better, but we need to talk about issues that are important to both of us, and especially to our children." Narcissists, when unsure about where the conversation is headed, will want to know everything immediately. However, that does not mean it's ready, set, go—on the narcissist's terms. You will still need to use a pre-emptive strike to declutter the conversation of all denying, defensive, or demeaning interruptions. For face-to-face or phone conversations, the preemptive strike may begin like this: "I'd like to propose some ground rules: When one of us speaks, the other listens. We will each be mindful of the time we speak so the listener can reflect and have a chance to respond. I'd also like to suggest that, while we both might get triggered during this conversation, we refrain from disrespecting one another; erupting into anger, threats, or criticalness; or abruptly storming out or hanging up. If we reach a point of escalation, let's agree to pause the conversation and come back to it. Does that seem fair? Would you like to add anything to the ground rules?"

If the narcissist is snarling, has left the room midway through your statement, or hung has up, do not despair. Move on to the trusty voice-recording app on your phone and return to the confrontation like this: "It's sad that we cannot talk constructively as co-parents, when we both love our children and want the best for them. Clearly, the triggers are unbearable, as just evidenced in this recent interaction. [This part holds him accountable for his maladaptive reactions to his narcissistically injured ego.] So, instead, I'll record my thoughts and requests. You can then listen at your convenience and take some time to consider your response without the distracting emotional conflict that occurs when we communicate live."

You might also say: "I hope you can hear this in the spirit intended, which is to reconfirm our agreements and values regarding [fill in the blank: scheduling, dating relationships, discipline of the children, or something else]. I do not intend to be critical of you, to make you the bad guy, or to alienate you from the children. Their relationship with both of us is important. But it cannot come at any cost. Right now, I feel they are paying too high an emotional price when you change their schedule at the last minute, or when they get to your house—as they did last week—and find your new friend sleeping over. We both have the right, of course, to have a life. But they are young, vulnerable, and confused. They need us to consider the time for healing and adjusting. Surely you must agree that we both need to be thoughtful about how we expose them to new people and changes in our lives now. I look forward to working on this together. I know you love them."

Yes, yes—a little gag may follow. And there is no guarantee that the narcissistic co-parent will grace you with the respect of a thoughtful response. But he will hear you, and, once again, you're planting seeds that you'll see grow into behavior patterns. Tending to this garden is tedious. It takes enormous stamina to cultivate a small but meaningful harvest amid decades of overgrowth. And, when all else fails, you may need to go back to strategy 1 in this section and seek legal assistance.

STRATEGY 3: LISTEN CAREFULLY AND SEEK PROFESSIONAL HELP WHEN NEEDED

Your child must have at least one healthy, open-minded, open-hearted, and open-armed listener, comforter, empathizer, and soother. Encounters with the narcissistic parent, and the shuffling back and forth between homes, can cause emotional fatigue, confusion, isolation, instability, and compromised self-worth. Encourage your child to talk with you. Though you may experience your own agony with your child's struggles, your compassionate and resilient presence will allow your child to release the pressure valve on their pent-up frustration.

Apply thoughtful disciplinary consequences and set limits on egregious acting-out behaviors that may be linked to your child's frustrations. Other options include suggesting that they try finding some relief by yelling into a pillow, banging a drum, or role-playing with puppets (great for small children). You could also propose running or other forms of exercise, since movement can be a great exterminator of angst.

If your child expresses fear or depression, acts out excessively, or demonstrates a radical change in behaviors, it might be time to consult a child or family therapist. By speaking with a family therapist together with your child, whether in family therapy or as an advocate for your child in individual therapy, you continue your role as comforter and advocate for your child as you seek additional guidance.

Conclusion

Some of you may worry that your child will grow up with low self-worth and will have the tendency to gravitate toward life partners who are similar to their narcissistic parent—emotionally volatile, detached, critical, and controlling. You worry that they may subjugate their own preferences and needs to maintain peace and stability, overfocus on their achievements as the only way of feeling like they matter, or become narcissistic themselves.

While these are feasible outcomes, it is not likely to happen to a child who is supported by one parent's fierce commitment to nurturing, (healthy) limit setting, empathy, unconditional love, praise and encouragement, modeling attuned presence, and perfectly imperfect humanness. You are the weary warrior who repairs the ruptures caused by the narcissistic co-parent, seeking help when needed and confronting the battle when thorny engagement or legal help is necessary.

It's not fair. You should not have to carry this healthy parenting burden alone. You will have missteps, charged moments, and angst to manage. You will need to attend to your own emotional needs, ensuring that you give that fundamental nutrient to your child—one stable and sturdy parent.

In this chapter, you've been exposed to myriad strategies for helping your children (and yourself) better cope with the narcissistic parent's behaviors. Your aim is to spare your children from blame for the alienating, scolding, demanding, and dismissive ways of the narcissistic parent. Your mission is to be reliably nurturing and reparative. You will use leverage and legal support with your narcissistic co-parent when necessary, anticipate glitches and timing to the best of your ability, and pause when escalations occur. You will empathically confront, craft intentional language, and install "we" phrases for efficacious outcomes.

You are the experimental emotional gardener, "dropping the seeds in the soil." You've seen examples and strategies that may resonate with your own experiences, and hopefully either confirm you're on the right track or embolden you with new ways of addressing complex issues with your narcissistic co-parent, and with your children.

In the final chapter, I'll guide you through strategies that will further accessorize your new linguistic ensemble. Previous points will be reiterated, elaborated, and tailored to fit your needs.

CHAPTER 9

Making the Most of a Difficult Situation:
Seven Gifts of Communication with a Narcissist

The artist is nothing without the gift, but the gift is nothing without work.

—Émile Zola

Each of us has a personal communication style. It stems from our temperament, and adopted and practiced skills, and is funneled through language, gestures, expressions, and behaviors, as a means of relating to and connecting with others. The gifts of communication discussed in this chapter are nothing like the "gift of gab," or going on and on about anything. They are the benefits of authentic communication appropriate to the context and undertaken with integrity. They are the gifts you offer to others when you communicate thoughtfully and carefully, with attention to not just what you're saying but also how you're saying it.

Just as the word "gift" has several meanings, the gifts of communication with a narcissist exist on various levels. A gift can be either something voluntarily given or the very act of giving. "Gift" can also refer to natural qualities or capabilities, such as an innate forte for touching the hearts and souls of others through language. However, a talent can also be developed through practice and intention. Gifted communicators are people who have cultivated a facility for listening to their inner wisdom and making sense of their lives, just as you've done throughout this book. Gifted communicators know the value of observing, listening, and probing the world beyond their own skin. They express themselves and engage in dialogue with elegance, grace, empathy, and thoughtfulness. The good news is that we can all develop this talent.

Conversational Narcissist

Unfortunately, most narcissists do not develop this talent for "gifted" communication. Although some may be great orators or charismatic, most narcissists have conversations to bring attention to themselves; win approval, status, and recognition; or to control opinions, decisions, and outcomes. They will wait impatiently for you to pause so they can interject something (relevant or not) about themselves. They are unapologetically interruptive, poor listeners, and nonreciprocal in the dialogue, meaning they take little notice of what you are saying, except as it pertains to them. Conversation with a narcissist is hardly an exchange of ideas or feelings. It's a one-way delivery, a monologue, a lecture, a scolding, a pompous orating, a brainy self-indulgent idea, an attention-seeking point of view, or a command.

Communication as an Art Form

By now, you've learned a great deal about yourself, and about you in relation to the narcissist in your life. You have new wisdom and have learned and honed skills for embracing the present and distinguishing between truth and fiction. You have a new awareness and perhaps more empathy, enabling you to peel back the layers of the narcissist to find the vulnerable, lonely soul at the core. You can stand up for yourself without being defensive because you feel no need to defend. You can make a thoughtful request without resorting to a counterattack. You can anticipate imperfect and even unsettling moments, and accept this possibility with less angst because you can repair these interactions and care for your own wellness. You're unburdened by knowing that none of us have the authority or even ability to change someone else. You've developed skills of self-expression and attuned listening that serve to create a positive impact, wedging open a new space where change might occur. You can drop those seeds and cultivate a potential harvest with your new strategies. You are poised to share your gifts through a personally crafted art of communication.

Harnessing the Force

Perhaps you know the phrase "May the Force be with you" from Star Wars. The Jedi knights suggest that a sentient, interplanetary energy lies within us all, binding us together and giving us the power to withstand opposition and create light in moments of darkness. I'd like to suggest a similar approach, captured by the acronym FORCE, which stands for flexibility, openness, receptivity, competence, and enlightenment.

When engaged in this state of FORCE, your interactions will be more authentic and rewarding, and you can share your wisdom in a way that sheds a warm and brilliant light on darker moments. When interacting with difficult people, make use of your heightened empathy and sharpened focus to manifest the elements of the FORCE:

Flexibility: Adjust your statements, questions, and responses to fit the situation. Resist and discard rigid and unbendable inclinations and ideas.

Openness: Listen without judgment or expectations. Not jumping to conclusions allows discovery to occur, even while predictable patterns may still dominate.

Receptivity: Use eye contact, facial expression, and body language, combined with your words and tone of voice, to suggest that you are ready to relate to others and invite their ideas and feelings without coercion, interruption, or censorship. Use sturdy limit-setting when the narcissist violates boundaries with verbal and disrespectful replies.

Competence: Be a credible and empathic listener and display clarity and sensibility when communicating, along with enthusiastic and attuned listening. Be a role model of authenticity. Try not to be distracted or motivated by winning, self-righteousness, or approval-seeking from the narcissist.

Enlightenment: Be curious. Encourage and demonstrate interest in exchanging insights. Create an atmosphere of mutual awareness and understanding through spoken and unspoken language, shining light on the darkness of ignorance and inviting the narcissist to do the same for you.

Being self-possessed permits you to tap into your personal FORCE. But here's the irony: Effective communication, containing all the elements of FORCE, cannot be effective if it's *forced*. It must emerge as naturally and gracefully as leaves unfold in spring. Though your inner resources may seem difficult to access, they do lie within. If you have a self-sacrifice or subjugation schema, it's important to realize that becoming self-possessed doesn't mean becoming selfish. It simply means equalizing the ratio of giving and receiving—getting off the one-way street that leads to your disappearance and the narcissist's preeminence. Being self-possessed means being informed by an illuminated consciousness and steady confidence. It means becoming personally defined. Everything you've learned from this book, and from other resources, will guide the way.

If your new skills enable you to create a rewarding and reciprocal relationship with the narcissist, you'll undoubtedly feel an enormous burden has been lifted. A satisfying relationship is among the greatest of gifts life has to offer. In addition, your mastery of effective communication will assist you in other challenging interactions. After all, if you can successfully handle one of the biggest button pushers on the planet, you can handle almost anyone.

Presenting Your Gifts

You've now collected many tools for surviving and even personally thriving in a relationship with a narcissist. It won't be easy, but with time you'll learn to wield these tools more adeptly. Your tools—identifying schemas, anticipating difficult encounters, being mindful, engaging in self-reflection, directing a calming focus on the breath, using empathic confrontation, extending compassion, and all the others—are designed to integrate with each other to ignite your inner FORCE, invigorate your voice, and strengthen your stance as you encounter difficult interpersonal situations.

It's similar to playing tennis: You need to anticipate the other person's actions, move to be in position to respond, keep your eye on the ball, adjust your response, make strong and consistent contact with the ball, and follow through—and then be ready to do it all again. It takes practice to integrate these moves and skills into the well-choreographed synchronous flow that produces a satisfying shot.

Here are a few other, more general communication skills you can use to heighten the effectiveness of the skills you've been working on:

- **Matching impact to intention:** Craft what you say and how you say it so it's received as you intended. Keep in mind what you hope to communicate, and choose words and ways of expressing yourself that will ensure the other person receives the message you'd like to impart. For example, if you're aware that you're very angry but would primarily like to communicate that you feel lonely, you'll need to consciously express yourself in a way that communicates loneliness rather than anger. Anger sends out the alert that something "important" is happening behind the anger. Look for that feeling—it's looking for you to give it a voice.

- **Modeling:** Give the other person an example of what you expect in return. For example, if you speak calmly and respectfully, you'll have a better chance of getting the same in response. This is not easy with narcissists but, if consistent, it can have an impact.

- **Having reasonable expectations:** Know what your listener is capable of and know what you feel capable of in that moment. Some days are better than others for engaging in challenging communication. Listen to your mind and body, and choose your battles thoughtfully. Timing is a key ingredient for effective interactions.

Additionally, the seven gifts of communication detailed below will complement your craft and enrich all of your relationships—not just the difficult ones! Each gift is illustrated with a vignette, and although most of these vignettes describe interactions between couples, they are equally relevant to relationships with people other than a romantic partner. Also, keep in mind that for this artful employment of communication to be effective, you must come prepared with steady eye contact; a gently paced, confident, and clear voice; a patient ear; and, of course, the FORCE—a flexible, open, receptive, competent, and enlightened state of mind.

The Seven Gifts

By communicating with integrity and self-disclosure, you offer valuable gifts to those you interact with. Sharing yourself in this way will help you bolster your sense of self-worth—and help the narcissist in your life potentially do the same, and heal his inner child, which makes positive change possible. As you model these seven arts, the narcissist in your life may become a more effective communicator—perhaps first with mimicry and then with authentic exposure, thus closing the circle and allowing you to become the beneficiary of these same gifts. Of course, there are countless arts of communication, but for our purposes, these seven are the most relevant:

1. The art of mutual respect is an expression of the gift of generosity.

2. The art of self-disclosure is an expression of the gift of courage.

3. The art of discernment is an expression of the gift of truth.

4. The art of collaboration is an expression of the gift of shared effort.

5. The art of anticipating clashes is an expression of the gift of foresight.

6. The art of apology is an expression of the gift of responsibility.

7. The art of reflective listening is an expression of the gift of balance.

1. The Art of Mutual Respect

Mutual respect entails acknowledging differences without negative labeling. This is the gift of generosity. You accept the narcissist's different point of view without becoming critical, defending your position, or discarding your own opinions. You know that differences can set the stage for a long, drawn-out drama. You're aware that understanding something doesn't necessarily mean agreeing with it. You're committed to understanding, compromise, and mutual respect for one another's thoughts, beliefs, and desires. You expect the same in return.

Let's say your husband says, "I've decided on the landscaper I plan to hire this season," and you disagree. You reply conveying mutual respect: "I can understand how strongly you feel about hiring Mr. Landscaper, and I'd like to be considerate of that. I appreciate your effort in researching options. I know the beauty of the property is important to you. I'm open to your plan, but I'd like to discuss it further. I'm feeling conflicted because my friend's son is desperately in need of work, and I'd feel bad not giving him the job. I know it's risky, but I'd like to give him a chance. I hear he's very good. Can we think it through together? Perhaps you can help me to see why this may or may not be the best option." Should the narcissist respond in an entitled, impatient, or condescending manner, you can use the implicit assumption rule from chapter 7 (the benefit of the doubt) and establish reciprocity.

2. The Art of Self-Disclosure

Self-disclosure allows you to unburden yourself of withholding the truth. This is the gift of courage. Securely attached to your inner strength, you reveal your full self to the narcissist—without the use of gratuitous insult. Even though it often seems counterintuitive to expose your vulnerability to him, like trying to hug a snarling dog, you've learned that his bark is a protective device; perhaps he's more like a sheep in wolf's clothing. You don't divulge to make him feel like a terrible person, but to help him appreciate the impact of his behavior. When you are no longer willing to toil in the salt mines of passive nods, acceptance of character assaults, and hopeless resignation, this gift will liberate real communication.

Let's say that your partner comes home and growls, "I am sick of coming home and finding you on the phone. Look at this place. Where's today's mail? Would it kill you to be free to talk to me for a change? Oh, forget it."

You take a calming breath, then reply: "I know it makes you feel bad, as if you don't matter to me, when you get home and find me on the phone. I understand, and I'm sorry that it makes you feel that way. I look forward to seeing you, but I need some help knowing when you'll get home, since it varies. I also need you to know that when you speak to me this way, it hurts. I know you don't intend the words to hurt me, but they do. And when I feel hurt, it's difficult for me to feel and express love for you, even though I truly want that in our relationship. I typically just give in or pull away. I don't want to do that anymore. I'd like to work on this together and hope you'd like to as well."

3. The Art of Discernment

Schemas, which lie at the heart of narcissism and dealing with a narcissist, require discerning between the here and now versus the "there and then." This is the gift of truth. When you discern, you communicate with a clarity that's based in the present moment. You clear the cobwebbed obstacles of the past and enter the present. You acknowledge history without succumbing to it. Like most of us, the narcissist in your life is prone to letting memory's playbook guide the truth. You can help him distinguish reality from automatic beliefs and habits. Because you recognize the importance of paying attention and have been working on this skill, you are adroitly prepared to be the wake-up caller.

Let's say you've asked your partner what time he'd like to leave to go to his father's for dinner, and he says, "How many times have we been there now, about a hundred? You know damn well how long it takes to get there. Why are you bothering me with these ridiculous questions? I'm trying to finish this presentation for a very important meeting on Monday. You just don't seem to get how important this is to me, do you? I'd like to keep a roof over our heads, you know. There's a lot of pressure on me."

You keep a steady grip on the image of a little boy who was always trying to please his dad, only to be consistently met with his father's impatience, criticism or silence, and realize that your husband's response has nothing to do with you or your question. There's a certain incongruousness to his spouting. Though you're offended by his unkindness, you understand the power of his schemas. You keep yourself securely attached to the present and the truth. You look down the long corridor of your own historic emotional residence and see the little girl who would take the blame for anything if it meant keeping the peace at home. Your connection to that old reality has forged sensations in the present that pulse through your nervous system like a runaway train, but you recognize these are old, schema-driven responses.

So, you take a deep breath, calm yourself, and look at your partner bound by his fears. Then you say, "I know you're busy, but I need a few moments of your time. This relationship is important to me. You're right: we've made the trip many times and I know exactly how long it takes to get to your father's house. I understand the pressure you're feeling at work and the burden to maintain our lifestyle. You work very hard, and I appreciate everything you do. I guess I could have been more precise, and asked, 'Do you want to leave early to spend some time with your father before dinner?' I guess you could have just answered the question. Look at me, I know you and really get you. This is me—I'm not your dad. I imagine these encounters with your father can bring up all kinds of uncomfortable feelings , and you may not be aware of them. It must have been very difficult dealing with him all those years. I know you're trying to be closer to him now that he's marginally mellowed. Let's not let it spoil things between us."

If the situation remains heated, consider taking a time-out so both of you can cool down and self-reflect before reconvening.

4. The Art of Collaboration

Collaboration invokes the collective power of "we." This is the gift of shared effort. Though we make mistakes, we also have something to offer one another in working together. In a "we" state, your dialogue is carefully sculpted from the clay of shared responsibility. You're informed by the narcissist's extreme sensitivity to feeling defective and ashamed, his fear of being controlled and taken advantage of, and his inability to ask for connection. You know that he can launch into entitlement, grandiosity, bullying, or avoidance when his schemas are triggered. Being collaborative keeps finger-pointing at bay and helps keep the narcissist at ease.

Cognitive therapists and schema therapists use "we" language with clients to mediate hierarchical struggles in therapy. This means we offer clients our help identifying feelings and links between historical and current problems. We help them develop strategies in a way that invites them to understand, challenge, question, and have input. We aren't invested in power struggles. The goal of collaboration is to understand these issues and find mutually agreeable strategies for change.

When difficult feelings arise during therapy with narcissistic clients, I often say something like, "Wow, isn't the brain amazing? One minute you and I are immersed, with curiosity and compassion, in an important investigation of your history or your current challenges, and the next minute we're having uncomfortable feelings with each other. Hmm...let's look at this." Invoking the collective and acknowledging a shift in feelings assigns no blame or shame, freeing the narcissist to investigate the triggering event rather than resorting to self-destructive coping modes.

The collaborative approach is especially important with narcissists who are prone to buttoning up their vulnerability behind walls of self-protection. While you can't always predict what will trigger you and the narcissist in your life, you can artfully offer the gift of "we" when trying to communicate.

Let's say you decide to call your narcissistic mother and invite her to spend the day with you. She replies, "I would love to. But please don't take me to that abominable restaurant where we ate last time. I raised you to have better taste than that. And if you want to go shopping, you'd better plan on a late dinner. You know how difficult it is for you to make decisions and to find things that fit you. Frankly, I could be happy spending the day in the city, but you get so nervous there. Oh well, you can decide, dear. I'm sure it will be lovely."

You've worked hard at this relationship and mostly accept your mother's difficulty expressing her love. You have learned how to successfully maintain loving, healthy, and healing relationships with others. Before responding, you remind yourself that you love your mother, though you're not always sure why. You hold on to reasonable expectations and a sense of humor. You wrap a loving imaginary arm around the pained heart of little you. You peer into the origins of your mother's narcissism and know she loves you, even if she bumbles most of the time. With that, you say, "Mom, look how difficult it is for us to ask for what we need from each other. It doesn't really matter to me how we spend the time. I just want to spend it with you. It's amusing and a bit sad how uncomfortable we get with each other's choices and styles. We need to find a better way to ask for what we need, instead of getting annoyed and critical with each other. If I were to start over, I'd tell you it doesn't matter what we do, but I'd love to spend some time with you. And if what we do matters to you, which is truly fine, we could come up with a plan that suits us both. It would probably be a lot easier and more honest that way. What do you think? How about we give this another try?"

5. The Art of Anticipating Clashes

Anticipating clashes allows you to preempt the pitfalls in your relationship. This is the gift of foresight. The brain, in part, offers this gift. You are endowed with the ability to draw upon memory to predict what lies ahead. For example, you may know someone so well you can finish their sentences. Or how about your memory of the sharp bend in the road on your route to work? It's memory that reminds you to slow down there to avoid losing control of your car. It is the wisdom of what-if and the memory of how-to that keeps you safe. We have a seemingly infinite number of memories that allow us to preempt trouble without even thinking about it. Adding your mindfulness skills to this innate gift, you have not only the wisdom of experience, but a robust repertoire of on-the-spot reflexes. In your interactions with the narcissist in your life, you can rebuild the very foundation on which your communications are based.

Let's say you haven't seen your father in months. He's invited you to lunch, but at the last minute, he calls to cancel for the third time because of his usual work-related priorities. He says, "I'm afraid that I'm going to have to cancel our lunch date again, sweetie. It's work. I have this client who...blah, blah, blah. I could have refused to meet with him, but...yada yada, and, well, you know your old man [chuckle]. Now don't go getting sulky with me. I'll call you soon. Okay, I gotta go."

You saw this coming. You've experienced this pattern over many years. Your father has rarely kept promises to spend time with you. He only seems motivated to see you when you're about to make a big life decision without his magnanimous advice. These meetings make him feel important—fatherly, in his mind. And, while you appreciate his input—he is a very bright guy, after all—you'd like to feel that he's interested in other parts of you and your life. You have pretty much given up your expectations, but not your longings. You want to keep him in your life, perhaps for your children, perhaps even a little bit for you. But you'd like to do so without resentment.

Unfortunately, dealing with him isn't like the sharp bend in the road on the way to work. You've been unable to figure out a way to steer clear of the convolutions in your relationship and hold on to yourself—until now. With your gift of anticipating clashes combined with some preemptive measures, you can respond to your dad with a secure voice and without blaming, attacking, or sulking. You are aware (more than he is) that he harbors a profound sense of inadequacy and has an emotionally vacant communication style. You know that he overcompensates for his sense of inadequacy through his work and competitiveness, and you know he can become defensive when confronted. You also know that he needs time to synthesize information and doesn't respond well in the moment.

With this knowledge and experience, you reply, "Dad, before you hang up, I'd like to ask for a few moments of your time. I know this may hurt your feelings. I know you're sensitive to my opinion of you and that you care very much about me. I know how important your work is to you and how everyone in the family has benefited from your success. I'm grateful for that. But I'd really like to have some time with you, just hanging out for no special reason. Maybe we could just talk. I know that you aren't very fond of 'touchy-feely' talk, as you call it, but I miss you, and I'm disappointed when you cancel our dates. I'd appreciate it if you could show me more consideration by giving me a little notice. I had to make special arrangements, which I can't change now, in order to see you. I'm not blaming you, Dad. I'm simply asking you to think about the impact on me. I don't want you to feel guilty, but I wish you understood how I feel. You don't have to respond right now. I know that you're pressed for time. Thanks for listening."

6. The Art of the Apology

A genuine apology places emphasis on compassion for the wounded, not redemption for the transgressor. This is the gift of responsibility. This is true remorse. With this gift, you are responsible for the impacts of your words, sentiments, and behaviors, especially when they're hurtful. You know that your behavior can serve as a model for the narcissist, and you hope for reciprocity. Therefore, you model an apology based in a compassionate understanding of how and why certain messages hurt him, in the hope that he'll learn how to offer an apology that reflects the same. You express authentically remorseful feelings that are free of self-loathing or a preoccupation with guilt. You are grounded in the experience of the other person, not focused on personal redemption. It's less about you than it is about your responsibility. You know you're fine, even when you make a mistake.

Let's say your boyfriend has a problem with people being late. He places a lot of importance on being prompt, largely because his socialite mother, who was unreliable and haphazard, occasionally forgot to pick him up after school, leaving him frightened and embarrassed. He can be unforgiving, even when unavoidable circumstances interfere with being on time. Therefore, you try to protect his inner child from experiences that would trigger these haunting feelings of fear and humiliation. You value promptness too and don't like to keep others waiting. But lately you've been distracted, stressed, and often running late, even with him. You know you've been careless, but you haven't been honest about it, and your boyfriend is clearly upset, although he doesn't say it.

So, you take the first step and say, "I'm sorry for the carelessness I've shown lately when it comes to being on time. I sense that you're upset with me, and I understand. Because I know your history and the issues with your mom, I know how it hurts you when people don't keep their word—especially me. I know how it made you feel forgotten and even foolish in the eyes of others when your mom wasn't responsible. But you aren't a fool, and I haven't forgotten you. It's my problem, and I'm committed to fixing it. I understand how my actions and excuses just keep hurting you. I'm sorry. I don't want to hurt you. While I can't promise that I'll never let you down in this relationship, I will do my best to be more attentive and thoughtful."

You expect only to be heard. Your intention is for your boyfriend to feel cared for. You know you aren't a bad person. You don't need to be stroked, and you don't need to punish yourself. You can hold yourself accountable for both the positive and negative contributions you make in your relationships. You expect the same from others. This approach offers an avenue for healing and is a model of what you expect from the narcissist when it's his turn to repair a tattered encounter. This is so difficult for the narcissist to do without professional help and/or good modeling to light the path. They struggle with that deep-down feeling of being flawed, defective, or the bad guy. An apology is like admitting that they are dirt; they are broken and deserve to be shamed. This is at the core of why they cannot easily apologize.

7. The Art of Reflective Listening

Reflective listening involves mirroring the communication of the other person and extracting hidden sentiments. This is the gift of balance. You know both how to articulate information and how to put self-interest aside and invite your listener to express himself. You are an ardent companion in communication who respectfully and patiently allows others to share themselves with confidence, knowing you'll meet them nonjudgmentally. You listen carefully and reflect an unbiased replay of what you hear, which clarifies and validates. You wait your turn to express your point of view.

Knowing how threatening honest communication can be for the narcissist, you extract hidden meanings and masked vulnerabilities by gently mirroring what you believe remains unspoken. You know that by listening and reflecting, you offer space for mutual discoveries, such as ways to avoid getting triggered; feelings about each other that have been closeted in anger, apathy, or avoidance; a strength you never knew you had; or a realization that the narcissist becomes receptive when he feels heard.

Let's say your partner has been suffering from a bad case of creative block and is dreading an upcoming meeting at work. Never particularly tolerant of frustration, she has become overly stressed and distracted. In desperation, she decides to put the pressure on a very unseasoned associate to write up the report. She arrives home from the dreaded meeting, sits down at the table, and begins to tell you about her terrible day, saying, "What a nightmare! How dare that little nobody-of-an-associate try to make me look incompetent at the meeting today. He's the incompetent one. His delivery was incomprehensible. My partners, my colleagues, hell, even my subordinates, were speechless when he gave that uninspiring report. He tried to lay it on me. Well, you better believe I let him have it. He's lucky to still have his job. Can you imagine? After all I've done for him, carrying him up the ladder. I knew I couldn't trust him. And don't you go telling me what I could have or should have done. I'm in no mood for your lectures and I don't want to talk about it."

There's a pause, and then she continues: "Didn't I tell you that I never should have let my partners talk me into bringing him into my division? I single-handedly took this marketing team to the top last year. Everyone there knows it too, even if they didn't have the nerve to say so in the meeting."

You've been listening quietly, eyes fixed upon her, even though she only occasionally looks directly at you. You felt the mild sting of her characterization of you: the lecturer, the "I told you so" partner. You place that on a mental shelf for now and remain a present and nondefensive listener. You can clearly see that your partner was unable to take responsibility for her poor judgment foisting the project on this novice associate. You shelve that too and remain a present and nonjudgmental listener.

But now that she's open to a reflective, extracting, and supportive response, you reply, "It's clear that you're feeling very upset. I know how hard you've worked and how unappreciated you've been feeling. I know it was a setback to have felt your creative stride off-balance last week, especially because you feel there's no one you can count on to share the burden. It sounds like it's hard, not receiving any backup from the team when you feel unfairly represented by a colleague. I can't imagine how difficult it would be for you to admit that you need help, especially since you take so much pride in your autonomy. I can sense your tension resonating in my own body as you describe the experience. Is there anything I can do to help?"

After more venting and some cooling down, you revisit parts of the conversation that were more relevant to your relationship: "I heard you say that you didn't want me to lecture you. I wonder if you truly feel that way or if it was just something you said because of how upset and embarrassed you were by the outcome of the meeting."

She clarifies that those statements were mostly due to being upset, but that sometimes she feels as though you lecture her. You accept her perception and ask her to point it out to you whenever it feels that way because you don't want her to experience you as uncaring or demeaning.

(There's no point in pursuing this point without evidence in the moment. It just becomes a "No, I didn't" "Yes, you did" conflict.)

The next item is a bit trickier. You reflect back that perhaps her anger is partly with herself for not living up to her own high standards. You gently point out that she's very demanding of herself and that this might make it hard for her to tolerate imperfection in others. You successfully resist feeding her insatiable cravings for admiration and instead nourish her with your appreciation for her honesty, enthusiasm, and untiring dedication to her goals, granting her permission to drop her guard and rest her head on your shoulder every now and then. By offering her this gift of communication, you also model your expectation for reciprocity. From here you create an unspoken invitation to pick up the cue and learn how she might listen to you too.

Conclusion

This chapter described seven gifts inherent in effective communication and the interpersonal arts. When you use these arts to express yourself with integrity, from a state of mind that's flexible, open, receptive, competent, and enlightened, your own personal FORCE is indeed with you. You are sturdy and stable on the high road. You are no longer willing to be dragged into the go-nowhere, low-road miseries.

Artfully applying these gifts of communication will promote interactions that are healthier, more satisfying, and more intimate. And as you craft your speaking and listening with thoughtfully chosen words, tone of voice, pacing, eye contact, facial expression, and body language, you'll be modeling what you'd like in return. Having a voice that accurately represents you and your intentions is always positive and beneficial. Sometimes this has to be enough. There are no guarantees and no sure paths to influencing change. Narcissists typically aren't the sort of people who voluntarily seek help, coaching, or any kind of assistance with breaking down their impenetrable emotional walls. If anything, they avoid this type of interaction at almost all costs, whether through adamant refusal, mockery, externalizing blame, or various forms of distraction and hiding.

But you've learned how you can play a vital role in opening the door to change, through leverage if need be, or perhaps just by offering kindness and compassion. No matter what the narcissist serves up, you can play a significant role in your own liberation from fear, intimidation, subjugation, self-sacrifice, and even abuse. You do this by identifying the life themes and schemas of your early experience, paying attention to triggering events and internal cues, setting limits, and adapting your responses to both the narcissist and your own automated inner dialogue. Liberating this healthy, wise, and awakened self within you is perhaps the ultimate achievement, leading to healthy and thoughtful (albeit not easy) choices.

The strategies in this book have the potential to be highly effective tools in bringing about more satisfying experiences with a narcissist. However, the journey can be both lonely and arduous. Sometimes the help of a professional therapist can be of tremendous value. Schemas can be very rigid and sometimes impenetrable, despite your best efforts. Should you choose to seek professional assistance, I recommend you find someone versed in the foundations of cognitive behavioral therapy and trained in schema therapy. In the Resources section, you'll find contact information for organizations that can help you find a therapist.

Acknowledgments

I would like to acknowledge the following people, whose love, patience, guidance, and support carried me through this process. I could not have written this book without you.

Momma, you have given me so much strength and the courage to believe in myself. My beautiful Samya "Sweet Pea," you are the light of my life; you are a truly amazing human who brings so much joy to me and to others. My other "kiddo" treasures: Rachel and Ben, Andrew, Mike, and Emily, ever so special to me. My husband, my dearest David, I am so lucky to have your constant love and encouragement. My dear sister, Lisa (Shmish); brother-in-law, Arthur (Bro); and special niece, Cailin (MMGB)—thank you for your constant care and devotion. To all of my family members, you are so dearly cherished. My California "Miller" family—thank you for your support and your love. Jack Lagos, thank you for helping me make sense out of my life. What a gift you are.

Dr. Aaron T. Beck, how important your contribution to this field— the enormity of your impact is immeasurable. You provided me with an extraordinary foundation in this often-complicated profession, giving me a grounded philosophy in which to base my practice.

My dear friend (and mentor), Jeff Young, you have been my greatest inspiration. Your generosity is felt in infinite ways. I have learned so much because of you and your incomparable talent. You've given me not only a brilliant model for working with clients, but also an immense collection of cherished memories. "Sweet William" Zangwill, you are always there for me with empathy, thoughtfulness, and the perfect metaphor. My dear friend Cathy Flanagan, your soothing voice and warm heart seem to always show up just when I need them. Michael First, thank you for your supportive enthusiasm, friendship, and impeccable diagnostic skills. Dan Siegel, mentor and charismatic educator, you've shared your gentleness, sheer magic, brilliant insight, and lovely sense of humor, along with your unique gift for making dense and difficult material come alive in my brain.

My dear family of colleagues and affiliates of the Cognitive Therapy Center and Schema Therapy Institutes of New Jersey, NYC, and DC, thank you for tolerating my ups and downs, whining, and celebrating. How fortunate I am to be surrounded by such incredibly generous, bright, and compassionate people like you: Kathleen Newdeck, Robin Spiro, Kathy Kobberger, Lissa Parsonnet, Harriet Achtentuch, Jeff Conway, Travis Atkinson, Paul Schottland, Irv Finklestein, Liz Lacy, Carlos Rojas, Judy Margolin, John Gasiewski, Kathy Rudlin, Carolee Kallmann, Luke Rockwood, Scott Shapiro, Offer Maurer, Marsha Blank, Mary Burke, Margaret Miele, and Barbara Levy.

Joan Farrell and Ida Shaw, my soul sisters and creative collaborators, you are so dear to me. Rich Simon, you invited me to write a piece for *Psychotherapy Networker* on this subject, and look what happened! You will always be remembered as an incredible editor who consistently inspired and encouraged my confidence as a writer.

Tesilya Hanauer, not only did you ask me to write a book for you, but you were also continuously there beside me with enthusiasm, support, and brilliant input, never compromising the integrity of my work. This book would not have happened without your initiation and thoughtfulness. Nicola Skidmore and Clancy Drake, along with Tesilya, your superb editing, suggestions, and overall accommodating support have been so immensely appreciated. Jasmine Star, how lucky I am to have been assigned such a warm, talented, and energetic copy editor. You kept my spirits high throughout what is typically a very daunting task. You are a class act! And just when I thought I couldn't get any luckier…Jean Blomquist, my third edition copy editor, a dream come true. With a keen eye, thoughtful input, and utmost respect for my voice—every one of your suggestions just made it better. Thank you!

Dorothy Smyk, so grateful for all your incredible effort with translations and book sales! And to all of the staff of New Harbinger Publications and others who worked hard to make my book a success, my deepest thanks.

To the rest of my family and friends, my colleagues here and abroad—I am so blessed to have the many fortunes of your love and wisdom. And finally, thank you to my clients: there are so many of you who have been a major source of inspiration to me and to my professional development. I am so grateful for your confidence in me, and for the unparalleled privilege of knowing your stories and witnessing your courage. I am in awe of you. Your openness and your commitment to the painstaking and exhilarating path to personal healing and renewal forever reminds me of why I chose to work in this field.

The revisions and new material in this third edition were written with endless gratitude for my International Society of Schema Therapy family. Your inspiration and constant support keep the ideas flowing and the creative candle glowing.

Finally, I would also like to express my immense gratitude to the many readers who have taken the time to write me, offering appreciation, feedback, keen questions, and even critically challenging points of view. All of your thoughtful insights and heartfelt stories have contributed to this third edition of *Disarming the Narcissist*. I thank you for inspiring me to add new and relevant material and elaborations on helpful strategies. I hope you find this edition of the book informative and helpful, and I look forward to your continued feedback.

Resources

Organizations

The centers listed below offer a full range of services to individuals, couples, families, and groups seeking consultation or psychotherapy services. They also provide referrals, ongoing professional supervision, training in schema therapy, and graduate and postgraduate training in cognitive behavioral therapy. In addition, they host skilled speakers who are available for off-site seminars and workshops.

The Cognitive Therapy Center of New Jersey (Springfield, NJ). The center's director also provides supervision and training to professionals who are interested in learning about interpersonal neurobiology: https://disarmingthenarcissist.com/workshops-seminars/; (973) 218-1776; wendy.behary@gmail.com.

The Schema Therapy Institutes of NJ-NYC-DC, located in New Jersey: https://disarmingthenarcissist.com/workshops-seminars/.

Dr. Dan Siegel has a website offering information on interpersonal neurobiology and parenting, along with many helpful links: https://drdansiegel.com/

Susan Stiffelman's website offers podcasts, resources, and online membership communities for parenting, including Co-Parenting with a Narcissist: Susan Stiffelman and Wendy Behary; https://susanstiffelman.com/.

Dr. Jill Manning has a digital downloads page on her website dedicated to support those experiencing betrayal trauma: https://drjillmanning.com /digital-downloads/.

The Gottman Institute, located in Seattle, Washington, offers workshops for couples and training for professionals: https://www.gottman .com/; (888) 523-9042.

The National Domestic Violence Hotline: https://www.thehotline.org; (800) 799-7233, (800) 787-3224 (TTY).

Recommended Reading

Beck, A. T. 1991. *Cognitive Therapy and the Emotional Disorders.* London: Penguin Books.

Beck, A. T., A. Freeman, and D. D. Davis. 2006. *Cognitive Therapy of Personality Disorders.* New York: The Guilford Press.

Beck, J. S. 2005. *Cognitive Therapy for Challenging Problems: What to Do When the Basics Don't Work.* New York: The Guilford Press.

Behary, Wendy. 2020. "The Art of Empathic Confrontation and Limit Setting." In *Creative Methods in Schema Therapy: Advances and Innovation in Clinical Practice,* edited by G. Heath and H. Startup, chapter 14. London: Routledge Publications.

Behary, Wendy. 2013 (July/August). "Challenging the Narcissist: How to Find Pathways to Empathy." *Psychotherapy Networker.*

Behary, Wendy. 2012. "Schema Therapy for Narcissism." In *The Wiley-Blackwell Handbook of Schema Therapy: Theory, Research, and Practice,* edited by M. van Vreeswijk, J. Broersen, and M. Nadort. Chichester, West Sussex, UK: John Wiley & Sons.

Behary, Wendy. 2010 (May/June). "In Consultation: The Way to Say It... Taking on Some of the Most Challenging Moments in the Treatment Room." *Psychotherapy Networker.*

Behary, Wendy. 2006 (March/April). "The Art of Empathic Confrontation: Working with the Narcissistic Client." *Psychotherapy Networker.*

Behary, Wendy, and D. D. Davis. 2014. "Narcissistic Personality Disorder." In *Cognitive Therapy of Personality Disorders,* 3rd ed., edited by A. Beck, D. Davis, and A. Freeman, chapter 14. New York: The Guilford Press.

Behary, Wendy, and E. Dieckmann. 2013. "The Art of Adaptive Re-Parenting in the Treatment of Narcissism." In *Understanding and Treating Pathological Narcissism,* edited by John S. Ogrodniczuk. Washington, DC: American Psychological Association.

Behary, Wendy, and E. Dieckmann. 2011. "Schema Therapy for Narcissism: The Art of Empathic Confrontation, Limit-Setting, and Leverage." In *The Handbook of Narcissism and Narcissistic Personality Disorder: Theoretical Approaches, Empirical Findings, and Treatments,* edited by W. Keith Campbell and Joshua D. Miller, chapter 40. Hoboken, NJ: John Wiley & Sons.

Behary, Wendy, and E. Dieckmann. 2010. "Schematherapie: Ein Ansatz zur Behandlung narzisstischer Persönlichkeitsstörungen." *Fortschritte der Neurologie-Psychiatrie* 83: 463–78.

Bennett-Goleman, T. 2001. *Emotional Alchemy: How the Mind Can Heal the Heart.* New York: Three Rivers Press.

Campbell, W. K., and J. D. Miller, eds. 2011. *The Handbook of Narcissism and Narcissistic Personality Disorder: Theoretical Approaches, Empirical Findings, and Treatments.* Hoboken, NJ: John Wiley & Sons.

Fortgang, L. B. 2002. *Living Your Best Life: Ten Strategies for Getting from Where You Are to Where You're Meant to Be.* New York: Jeremy P. Tarcher.

Goleman, D. 2007. *Social Intelligence: The New Science of Human Relationships*. New York: Bantam Books.

Goleman, D. 1997. *Emotional Intelligence: Why It Can Matter More Than IQ*. New York: Bantam Books.

Gottman, J. M. 2002. *The Relationship Cure: A 5-Step Guide to Strengthening Your Marriage, Family, and Friendships*. New York: Harmony Books.

Gottman, J. and Silver, N. 2015. *The Seven Principles for Making Marriage Work: A Practical Guide from the Country's Foremost Relationship*. New York: Harmony Books.

Gottman, J. and Silver, N. 2013. *What Makes Love Last?: How to Build Trust and Avoid Betrayal*. New York: Simon and Schuster.

Layden, M. A. 2010. "Pornography and Violence: A New Look at the Research." In *The Social Costs of Pornography: A Collection of Papers*. Princeton, NJ: Witherspoon Institute.

Malkin, C. 2015. *Rethinking Narcissism: The Bad—and Surprising Good—About Feeling Special*. New York: Harper Perennial.

Mason, P. T. and Kreger, R. T. 2010. *Stop Walking on Eggshells: Taking Your Life Back When Someone You Care About Has Borderline Personality Disorder*. Oakland: New Harbinger Publications.

McBride, K. 2009. *Will I Ever Be Good Enough?: Healing the Daughters of Narcissistic Mothers*. Miami: Atria Books

Ogrodniczuk, J. S., ed. 2012. *Understanding and Treating Pathological Narcissism*. Washington, DC: American Psychological Association.

Siegel, D. J. 2012. *The Whole-Brain Child: 12 Revolutionary Strategies to Nurture Your Child's Developing Mind*. New York: Bantam Books.

Siegel, D. J. 2010. *Mindsight: The New Science of Personal Transformation*. New York: Bantam Books.

Siegel, D. J. 2007. *The Mindful Brain: Reflection and Attunement in the Cultivation of Well-Being.* New York: W. W. Norton.

Siegel, D. J. 2001. *The Developing Mind: How Relationships and the Brain Interact to Shape Who We Are.* New York: The Guilford Press.

Siegel, D. J., and M. Hartzell. 2013. *Parenting from the Inside Out: How a Deeper Self-Understanding Can Help You Raise Children Who Thrive.* 10th anniversary ed., New York: Jeremy P. Tarcher.

Skeen, M. 2011. *The Critical Partner: How to End the Cycle of Criticism and Get the Love You Want.* Oakland, CA: New Harbinger Publications.

Stiffelman, S. 2015. *Parenting with Presence: Practices for Raising Conscious, Confident, Caring Kids* (an Eckhart Tolle edition). Novato, California: New World Library.

Stiffelman, S. 2012. *Parenting Without Power Struggles: Raising Joyful, Resilient Kids While Staying Cool, Calm, and Connected.* New York: Simon & Schuster.

Twenge, J. M., and W. K. Campbell. 2009. *The Narcissism Epidemic: Living in the Age of Entitlement.* New York: Free Press.

Van Vreeswijk, M., J. Broerson, and M. Nadort, eds. 2012. *The Wiley-Blackwell Handbook of Schema Therapy: Theory, Research, and Practice.* Chichester, West Sussex, UK: John Wiley & Sons.

Young, J. E. 1999. *Cognitive Therapy for Personality Disorders: A Schema-Focused Approach.* Sarasota, FL: Professional Resource Press.

Young, J. E., J. S. Klosko, and M. E. Weishaar. 2006. *Schema Therapy: A Practitioner's Guide.* New York: The Guilford Press.

Young, J. E., and J. S. Klosko. 1994. *Reinventing Your Life: The Breakthrough Program to End Negative Behavior...and Feel Great Again.* New York: Plume.

References

Brown, N. W. 2001. *Children of the Self-Absorbed: A Grown-Up's Guide to Getting Over Narcissistic Parents*. Oakland, CA: New Harbinger Publications.

Giesen-Bloo, J., R. van Dyck, P. Spinhoven, W. van Tilburg, C. Dirksen, T. van Asselt, I. Kremers, M. Nadort, and A. Arntz. 2006. "Outpatient Psychotherapy for Borderline Personality Disorder: Randomized Trial of Schema-Focused Therapy vs. Transference-Focused Therapy." *Archives of General Psychiatry* 63(6): 649–58.

Goleman, D. 2007. *Social Intelligence: The New Science of Human Relationships*. New York: Bantam Books.

Gottman, J., and N. Silver. 2004. *The Seven Principles for Making Marriage Work*. New York: Orion.

Hotchkiss, S. 2003. *Why Is It Always About You? The Seven Deadly Sins of Narcissism*. New York: Free Press.

Iacoboni, M. 2009. *Mirroring People: The New Science of How We Connect with Others*. New York: Farrar, Straus and Giroux.

Manning, J. 2021. "What Is Betrayal Trauma?" https://drjillmanning.com/betrayal-trauma/.

O'Donohue, J. 2000. *Eternal Echoes: Celtic Reflections on Our Yearning to Belong*. New York: Harper Perennial.

Scruton, R. 2010. "The Abuse of Sex." In *The Social Costs of Pornography: A Collection of Papers*. Princeton, NJ: Witherspoon Institute.

Siegel, D. J. 2001. *The Developing Mind: How Relationships and the Brain Interact to Shape Who We Are*. New York: The Guilford Press.

Siegel, D. J. 2007. *The Mindful Brain: Reflection and Attunement in the Cultivation of Well-Being.* New York: W. W. Norton.

Siegel, D. J., and M. Hartzell. 2004. *Parenting from the Inside Out.* New York: Jeremy P. Tarcher.

Solomon, M. 1992. *Narcissism and Intimacy: Love and Marriage in an Age of Confusion.* New York: W. W. Norton.

Walsh, S. 2010. "20 Identifiable Traits of a Female Narcissist." June 28 blog post at *Hooking Up Smart.* Accessed November 30, 2012.

Wordsworth, W. 1892. *The Complete Poetical Works of William Wordsworth.* New York: Thomas Y. Crowell.

Young, J. E., and J. S. Klosko. 1994. *Reinventing Your Life: The Breakthrough Program to End Negative Behavior...and Feel Great Again.* New York: Plume.

Young, J. E., J. S. Klosko, and M. E. Weishaar. 2006. *Schema Therapy: A Practitioner's Guide.* New York: The Guilford Press.

Wendy Terrie Behary, LCSW, is founder and clinical director of The Cognitive Therapy Center of New Jersey, and codirector of The Schema Therapy Institutes of NJ-NYC-DC. She is also a founding fellow of the Academy of Cognitive Therapy. She maintains a private practice, specializing in narcissism and high-conflict couples therapy.

Foreword writer **Jeffrey Young, PhD**, is coauthor of *Schema Therapy*, and founder and codirector of The Schema Therapy Institutes of NJ-NYC-DC.

Preface writer **Daniel J. Siegel, MD**, is author of *The Mindful Brain*, and associate clinical professor at the UCLA School of Medicine Center for Human Development.

Real change *is* possible

For more than forty-five years, New Harbinger has published proven-effective self-help books and pioneering workbooks to help readers of all ages and backgrounds improve mental health and well-being, and achieve lasting personal growth. In addition, our spirituality books offer profound guidance for deepening awareness and cultivating healing, self-discovery, and fulfillment.

Founded by psychologist Matthew McKay and Patrick Fanning, New Harbinger is proud to be an independent, employee-owned company. Our books reflect our core values of integrity, innovation, commitment, sustainability, compassion, and trust. Written by leaders in the field and recommended by therapists worldwide, New Harbinger books are practical, accessible, and provide real tools for real change.

newharbingerpublications

MORE BOOKS from
NEW HARBINGER PUBLICATIONS

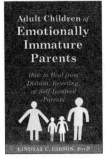